35

Social History of Canada

H.V. Nelles, general editor

GRACE MORRIS CRAIG

But This Is Our War

UNIVERSITY OF TORONTO PRESS

Toronto Buffalo London

© University of Toronto Press 1981
Toronto Buffalo London
Printed in Canada

ISBN 0-8020-2442-4

Canadian Cataloguing in Publication Data

Craig, Grace Morris.

But this is our war
(Social history of Canada, ISSN 0085-6207 ; 35)
ISBN 0-8020-2442-4
1. Craig, Grace Morris. 2. World War, 1914-1918 –
Personal narratives, Canadian.* 3. World War,
1914-1918 – Canada.* I. Title. II. Series.
D640.C72A4 1981   940.4'81'71   C81-094672-6

Social History of Canada 35

Publication of this book was assisted by a generous gift to the University of
Toronto Press from the Herbert Laurence Rous Estate.

Illustrations have been supplied by the author with the following exceptions:
from CANADIAN PACIFIC – *Metagama*; from PUBLIC ARCHIVES CANADA – field post
office PA-149, field kitchen PA-1596, resting in trenches PA-2468, on
Western Front C-30341 and PA-157, on *Olympic* PA-6049, Cobalt C-22035

Design by Antje Lingner, University of Toronto Press

For my grandchildren

In compiling this volume I am deeply indebted
to my editor Gerry Hallowell, and to my granddaughter
Moira Tasker, who insisted upon my undertaking it.

Contents

Introduction

H.V. NELLES

Was there ever a season more golden than the summer of 1914? Yes, of course there was. But none more intensely relived in memory. The radiance increased in the appalling darkness that followed.

Over 600,000 Canadians enlisted or were conscripted in the Great War. Casualties reached 230,000 by 1918. More than 60,000 soldiers, airmen, and nursing sisters died. Every third man was wounded; every tenth man was killed. Although the numbers are numbing, they cannot begin to convey the exhilaration, boredom, terror, and suffering of war. Colonel G.W.L. Nicholson's exemplary official history of the Canadian Expeditionary Force lays out the facts and circumstances of battle. But inevitably the individual soldier and the anxieties of the community he's from get lost in the bigger picture. The Great War levied a blood tax on almost every family in the country. Everyone knew someone at the front. As the cenotaphs in our towns attest, everyone knew someone who didn't return.

This book recalls the war through the experience of one family, the Morris family of Pembroke. It is really the story of a generation. Once these youngsters – Grace, Basil, and Ramsey Morris, Alf Bastedo, Gertrude Booth, Ambrose Moffat, Stuart Thorne, Bob Murray, Welland Williams – were carefree. Nearing the end of university, canoeing on the Ottawa River, testing themselves against the wilderness, looking out for new worlds to conquer, gazing off a mighty rock to a horizon that seemed limitless, these young people exuded energy, life, and hope. Then a distant war intruded. Responding to a primal duty they could not fully comprehend, the young men dropped their studies, left their Arcadian rambles behind them, and eagerly volunteered. Like thousands of others they left behind mothers and fathers, sisters, wives and lovers, who treasured every letter, waited anxiously for every battle to be reported in the newspapers, and dreaded the day when a telegram beginning 'regret to inform' might arrive. For the survivors and for those who fretted and toiled at home, life would never be the same again. In the mud and rain of Flanders a terrible burden of grief and guilt descended upon an entire generation. Through the nightmare the pre-war years of freedom and innocence glimmered and, for those who could remember, never faded.

Grace Morris Craig's memoir captures the bursting energy of one group of young Canadians suddenly caught up in the vortex of war. She was born in Pembroke on February 20, 1891. Her father, James Lewis Morris, and her mother, Mary Agnes Menzies, were both descendants of Scots who settled in the Ottawa Valley in the early nineteenth century. James, who had been the first graduate of the University of Toronto's School of Practical Science, had returned to his home town to set up an engineering firm specializing in railroad construction. The firm prospered and the family grew. A son, Ramsey, was born in 1893, and a second, Basil, arrived in 1895. Some of the joys of their childhood brighten the pages that follow.

Grace Morris attended Branksome Hall in Toronto, studied music and a bit of drawing, but was refused admission to the University of Toronto to study architecture on the grounds she was a woman. When the war came she threw herself into volunteer work in Pembroke and at the Peta-wawa military base nearby. Grace Morris was typical of the hundreds of thousands of women who exhausted themselves on the home front, organizing, sewing, fund-raising, working on assembly lines, entertaining, electioneering, keeping house, and waiting. And writing letters to her brothers and friends overseas. Her memories and the letters she received close the distance between the trenches and home, and recreate the anxieties that were felt so acutely at the time.

We should not have unrealistic expectations of letters home from the war zone. They do not provide as much direct testimony about trench life, about the hopes and fears of the soldiers, as one might expect. Military censorship precluded documentary detail. Both the writer of a letter and its receiver were engaged as well in a tacit conspiracy to cheer each other up. No language could convey the horrors. Things *were* beyond the imagination of those at home. And what would be the point of trying to describe the madness? No one dwelt upon morbid matters for long. As Alf Bastedo scribbled from the Ypres salient in 1915: 'One sees some rather dreadful sights in this place which it pays to forget about as quickly as possible and not to write about at all, so I try to remember only the nice things.'

Nevertheless, these letters are revealing in another sense. Note the absence of any hatred or malice towards the enemy. Observe the literary conventions that shape observation: the irony of natural beauty and man-made horror, the strange peacefulness of no man's land at night, and the clinging to memories of parting. Listen as different groups of British troops change the vocabulary of the Morris boys. These letters also reflect the gathering pride of a group of raw-boned Canadian lads discovering Britain, Europe, war, and the broader world of experience for the first time. Whether tunnelling, flying, repelling attacks or charging with bayonets, these young men discovered themselves and in these strange circumstances observed that Canadians *were* different and just as good at the arts of war as more practised hands. They all would have agreed heartily with Colonel C.P. Stacey's contention that the 'creation of the Canadian Corps was the greatest thing Canada had ever done.'

The Morrises were by no means a typical Canadian family. They were amongst a tiny minority who valued and could afford a university education. They were representatives of the small town commercial and professional bourgeoisie, which was just beginning to make connections through the schools, migrations, friendships, and professional careers of the children. Grace, Ramsey, and Basil came from a family that was a little better off and certainly better educated than most Canadian families. The children were more articulate and more widely travelled (within Canada) than most. Much of the pre-war optimism reflected in these pages stems from the privileged social position of the family; the thousands of unemployed workers who had to enlist to eat might not recall the years before the war with such wistful affection.

Nevertheless, their social class did not spare the Morris family grief. Through the letters from the front, through the trip Grace and her mother took to visit Ramsey and Basil on leave in England in 1916, the war was felt and understood in the Morris household with devastating immediacy. For the warriors, and for those who waited at home, the old life before the war took on new meaning as it receded. It, not the war, was the dream.

Grace Craig wrote this book for her grandchildren, the first generation of Canadians since 1914 to know a world without war. She wanted to tell them what it was like to be young long ago. With her lifelong love of history, she was inspired in part, she claims, by the example of Bernal Diaz del Castillo, who in the sixteenth century, at the age of eighty, wrote for his grandchildren his own eye-witness account of the conquest of Mexico under Cortes. Now in her nineties she still feels the need to explain, to a generation she hopes will never experience the pain, what it means to have the flesh and blood of one's generation ripped away.

Books like this complement the military histories and the scholarly studies of war. They remind us that battalions, however large, are ultimately made up of individuals, from families, all of whom make a sacrifice in the act of going to war. Grace Craig has composed a moving and exhilarating account of the Great War, an account that fathoms the emotional impact of that war on one family. Her memories speak of the sacrifice and the achievements of her generation.

SOME FURTHER READING ABOUT CANADIANS AND THE GREAT WAR

Colonel G.W.L. Nicholson's *Canadian Expeditionary Force, 1914–1919* (Ottawa 1964) is an essential starting point for anyone interested in the Great War. It should be supplemented with memoirs such as this and Will R. Bird's *Ghosts Have Warm Hands* (Toronto, Vancouver 1968). Three recent books cover the home front in quite different ways: Barbara Wilson's *Ontario and the First World War* (Toronto 1977), John Thompson's *The Harvests of War* (Toronto 1978), and Daphne Read's *The Great War and Canadian Society: An Oral History* (Toronto 1978). In *Canada and the Age of Conflict* (Toronto 1977) C.P. Stacey devotes two chapters to the diplomacy of the war. Robert Craig Brown's biography of *Robert Borden* (Toronto 1980) provides the most thorough and disciplined treatment of domestic politics in the period. The Great War has also supplied the setting for some notable fiction, including Charles Yale Harrison's *Generals Die in Bed* (1930; Hamilton 1975), and more recently Timothy Findley's *The Wars* (Toronto, Vancouver 1977) and Donald Jack's *The Bandy Papers*, now into a fourth volume. Readers interested in the literary conventions and backdrop of letters such as these will find Paul Fussell's *The Great War and Modern Memory* (London and New York 1975) illuminating – notwithstanding the fact that John McCrae, the Canadian soldier who wrote 'In Flanders Fields,' is identified as a British poet.

But This Is Our War

1 ❈ Then we were young ❈ ❈ ❈ ❈

'To grow up under the spell of a great river is a special blessing,' wrote the German writer Carl Zuckmayer in *A Part of Myself.* 'Birthplace is no fiction of the emotions, no intellectual construct. It governs growth and speech, sight and hearing; it animates the senses and opens them to the breath of the spirit ... Rivers sustain the land and keep the earth in balance ... It is along rivers that trade routes and languages meet. To be in the stream of things means to stand amid the fullness of life.' Zuckmayer was writing about the Rhine.

A river of equal beauty, with a spell of its own, is the Ottawa. Its waters come from lakes with beautiful-sounding Indian names like Capimitchigama and Timiskaming. From its source in the Canadian Shield it flows some seven hundred winding miles into the St Lawrence River at the island of Montreal: the ancient route of the voyageurs who tapped the fur wealth of the pays d'en haut, it was also the highway of escape to the wilderness for the coureurs de bois. Perhaps the Ottawa, with its long and unique history, has conferred a rich blessing upon all the children who grew up beside it, a blessing of vibrant memories.

From earliest childhood my brothers and I were aware of the river's history. One bright, sunny morning when I was very young my father awakened me and carried me to a window facing the Ottawa. I saw a large boom of logs drifting slowly down the centre of the still, wide river; on the top of the raft was a small house. 'This,' my father said, 'is the last square-timber raft to go down the Ottawa. This is a moment in history and perhaps you will remember.'

The big trees of the primeval forest were gone, but the forestry industry carried on. Each summer the 'sweep,' a large, flat-bottomed boat with bunks and a cook-house, arrived near our cottage at Fort William, on its way down from Deep River. After a storm many logs would be scattered along the shores, having jumped the booms in which they were being towed downriver to the mills. In two 'pickies,' red rowboats with pointed ends, the lumberjacks went about gathering up the stray logs. As children, the most exciting thing about the arrival of the 'sweep' was the cook, for he sometimes handed out big raisin cookies.

My family, originally from Scotland, had lived in Pembroke for several generations. James Morris, my grandfather, had come from his father's homestead at the eastern end of the new County of Renfrew to become the first sheriff when Pembroke was chosen as the county town. He had built a fine brick house near the courthouse with a superb view of Allumette Lake, the name given to the widening of the Ottawa River at Pembroke. In winter the river looked like a vast white plain stretching to the distant shore of Allumette Island, beyond which lay the low rounded range of the Laurentian Mountains, rich in shades of blue turning to purple in the evening light.

James' second son, my father James, was an imaginative boy, something of a dreamer. He watched with interest a party of young men measuring the land below his home along the edge of the river, and when he discovered they were gathering information for a railway line that would extend across the continent to the coast of British Columbia, he decided that he must be involved in this great enterprise. With his parents' permission he travelled to Toronto to enquire at the university about a proposed course in engineering. He found, to his intense disappointment, that the plans had been cancelled because no students had applied, and he was advised to enter a course in law or medicine. Though young and alone in a big city, the determination of his Scottish ancestors prevailed. For days he haunted the office of the registrar and finally won a promise that if he could find two more students a course in civil engineering would be started for them. This was accomplished, and a young man, John Galbraith, was appointed to be their teacher. In 1881 James became the first graduate of the School of Practical Science. After a summer with a survey party in the foothills of the Rockies, he joined the staff of engineers locating the new railway in the rough country north and east of Lake Superior, where one of his duties was to survey and lay out a site for a divisional point which was to be called Sudbury.

After several years with the Canadian Pacific Railway, my father returned to Pembroke to practise his profession there. He married Mary Menzies of Almonte, a lively, good-looking, young woman, daughter of the registrar of Lanark County.

There were three children. I was the eldest; Ramsey was two years younger; and two years younger still was Basil – the baby, as we called him, until he objected when reaching the age of three. We had a happy childhood. Our parents, though firm in matters of discipline, were kind and encouraged us in all our activities.

Our father was frequently away from home. Before the end of his career, at the age of eighty, the field of his activities extended to all of Ontario. While employed by the government after the war to study the lands of Ontario and the treaties with the Indians, he made an amazing discovery: the section of the province along Lake Ontario from Oshawa to Belleville, and including these two cities, had never been deeded to the Crown. Under his guidance this oversight was corrected in 1923.

My father was hopeful that his children would grow up with a feeling for the history of their country. He liked to tell us stories of his journey to Alberta and the foothills of the Rockies in 1881: how he had travelled by way of the United States, up the Missouri River, crossing the border to Fort Walsh in the Cypress Hills; how Calgary was a small group of log buildings, a fur trading post on the Bow River; how his survey party crossed the plains by horse and wagon, sometimes meeting groups of Indians on horseback, not knowing if they would be friendly. We loved these stories and begged to be allowed to handle the Indian souvenirs he showed us, the beaded things, and especially the tomahawk.

In winter a row of small evergreen trees stretched across the frozen whiteness of the river plain, marking the road that led from Pembroke on the Ontario side to Desjardins on the Quebec side. In summer a sturdy ferry-boat took the place of the icy road; it carried wagons and horses as well as people. When our grandfather from Almonte visited, he sometimes took my brothers and me for a ferry ride across the river, which we thought a great adventure.

During the summer months, many people of the town moved to cottages on sandy beaches or rocky islands. Upriver about twelve miles west of Pembroke, on the Quebec side across from Petawawa, was the ancient Hudson's Bay Company fur trading post of Fort William. In my day the mission church remained, standing in a field of wild flowers, weather-beaten but still intact. Sometimes a priest from the village of Sheenborough would come on Sundays to say mass, and the children would gather buttercups and daisies to decorate the altar. I enjoyed doing this and would be invited by my Roman Catholic friends to attend mass with them. It seemed a nice way to go to church, with the woodsy smell of nearby pine trees drifting in the open windows.

Along a crescent beach of yellow sand at Fort William was a row of cottages, partly hidden by tall red pines. Here Ramsey, Basil, and I spent long summers. We learned to swim and handle boats. My father made sure that we could paddle a canoe, which he assured us was a perfectly safe craft when properly handled. Sometimes he would put me in the bow of a canoe and take me out in a strong wind so that I would learn not to be afraid. The river did not always present a smiling face. Occasionally great storms originating in the Mattawa region came roaring down from the west, following the mountains and the river valley until they reached a peak at Lac Deschênes near Ottawa.

Every day in summer the steamer *Oiseau* stopped at our dock with mail and passengers on its way to Rapides des Joachims. Occasionally a picnic was organized to visit the great rapids, which were about forty miles to the west. One never grew tired of the solemn beauty of the river as the paddle-wheeler slipped past headland after headland following the base of the mountains. The drama of the day was provided by the sheer cliff Oiseau Rock, towering five hundred feet above the water. Sometimes the captain could be persuaded to sail close to the cliff and blow the whistle, sending volumes of sound echoing up and down the river. At midday the steamer arrived at Des Joachims, or 'Deswisha' as we called it. The walk over a shadeless rocky road to the rapids was exhausting but accepted by the pilgrims as a fitting part of the ceremony. Resting on huge boulders beside the thundering waters, the wayfarers communed with the Great Manitou, or possibly with the spirits of the voyageurs who had long ago passed that way.

At Pembroke the small, winding Muskrat River flowed into the Ottawa. A short distance up this river was a dam to provide waterpower for a flour mill, and in the winter the pond above the dam was a sheltered place for small hockey rinks. Groups of boys cleared the ice and maintained their separate rinks. As a result of their efforts, many excellent hockey players were produced, the most outstanding being Frank Nighbor, one of the first hockey stars in Canada.

Our mother was a warm, kind person with a wonderful sense of humour and many friends. Her dark eyes often sparkled with merriment, and I can still hear my father's admonition 'Minnie! Minnie!' when he sometimes thought her sense of fun had gone far enough. She found her home, husband, and children completely satisfying. Always having a competent servant, called 'the hired girl,' to help her, she had time to plan all the activities of the household and to entertain her friends.

My mother's helper for six or seven years was Emma, who had come from a farm in a township west of the town and brought with her a touch of German culture. She taught us, the children, singing games in German, 'Mit den Händen klap, klap, klap,' and the English nursery rhymes acquired a foreign sound, 'Vee Villie Vinkie.' A thing of beauty was the tree Emma decorated with tissue-paper garlands and flowers of many colours, which was brought secretly into the living room on Christmas Eve while we were having supper. When we rushed into the room, what a glorious sight it was, ablaze with tiny candles. My father made sure that a pail full of water was handy in case of an emergency. There was great regret in the family when Emma said goodbye and returned to the country to marry a clergyman.

Our house had one particularly beautiful room, which Basil later used to dream about when he felt lonesome while fighting in the trenches in France. It was a cheerful room with windows on three sides. Its white woodwork and ceiling and dark blue walls enhanced the gilt-framed family portraits and two large paintings done by my mother before she was married: well-executed copies of Landseer's study of two dogs and *Monarch of the Glen*, a picture of a handsome stag. A fire in the corner fireplace usually burned in the evenings. The round table in the centre and the bookcase desk, brought by my great-grandfather from Scotland, vied with an upright Steinway piano, given to me on my sixteenth birthday, to dominate the room.

At the age of six, after kindergarten held in a room over a store on Main Street, my real schooling began. A young woman, Miss Russell, came each day to teach me and my playmate Gertie Booth the three R's (reading, 'riting, and 'rithmatic). We had our lessons at the centre table in our living room. Gertie lived across the street in a brick house, larger than ours, with a tower on one of the corners. It had a garden with vegetables, flowers, and currant bushes and also a stable for a horse and a cow. The stable was brick like the house and very tidy but we were not allowed to go into it.

After two years of private lessons, Gertie and I were sent to public school, which was situated in the centre of the town. To reach it, we crossed by the stone bridge over the Muskrat River, a bitterly cold trip when a northwest wind blew down the Ottawa. Our first year at school was an unhappy experience as our teacher was nervous and bad-tempered, continually threatening the children with the strap – a large piece of heavy leather which she applied with vigour to the hands; there was much crying, though the boys, who were the usual victims, seldom broke down.

After the first year at school things improved. Our next teacher, Miss Carry Winters, was a strong, understanding woman, and under her direction I became a happy student. On reaching the second to last grade of public school, four of us were encouraged to try the examination for entrance to high school; all succeeded, two of us being at the top of the list in the county. The day the results were published happened to be the day of our Sunday School picnic when I won a prize for jumping. It was the first really exciting day in my life.

The high school in Pembroke, also in the centre of the town, contained four classrooms, a simple laboratory, and an assembly room on the top floor. The boys all took chemistry and physics, but in my year I was the only girl. Most of the girls took a course leading to teachers' training college; with the exception of nursing, that seemed to be the only profession open to women, unless a girl planned to continue her general education at the university. The only sport available to girls was basketball, which we played if we felt inclined but without instruction. Boys and girls shared the same classrooms but had separate playgrounds.

There was never any question as to how my brothers would be educated. At the University of Toronto Ramsey would enter an honours course for a Bachelor of Arts degree, preliminary to the study of law; and Basil would become an engineer to follow in his father's footsteps.

It was more difficult to decide what to do about their sister. At high school I had shown some ability as a student and my music teacher reported that I was the most promising of her pupils. This seemed to settle the matter. I would be educated in music. Nobody seemed to notice that much of my spare time was spent drawing – 'Gibson Girls' being my favourite subject.

My parents decided that at sixteen I was much too young to be alone in Toronto, so I was sent to a boarding school. Branksome Hall, the school chosen, had been founded by Miss Margaret Scott, one of my mother's teachers at the Ottawa Ladies' College. Quite a number of girls finished their education in boarding schools; they were frequently known as 'finishing schools' and much emphasis was put on deportment.

In those days, if you were a well-brought-up child, you did what your parents expected you to do. But from the beginning, in my case, I was happy to be in a girls' school, and quickly adapted to the routine. An excellent piano teacher was chosen for me and my programme was to spend many hours of practice every day to prepare for the University of Toronto examinations in piano. At the same time I entered the top form where a few girls were studying for 'honours matriculation' to the university. One of them, Alice Anderson, became my friend; later she graduated in medicine and became head of a hospital in India.

The subjects I chose for study were English, French, German, and history. There were also lectures in the history of art; it had been quite an accomplishment to gain permission to spend one afternoon a week in the painting and drawing class given by Miss Mattice of Hamilton, for Miss Scott seemed to think I would be wasting my time. It was thirty years later before my ambition to be a painter was fully realized.

Branksome Hall at that time was in a fine old house on Bloor Street East, now the site of the head office of the Manufacturers' Life Insurance Company. Behind the house were tennis courts and grounds that stretched to a lane running along the edge of the ravine. The lane, an extension of Collier Street, led to a stable where a few of the Branksome girls took riding lessons, using the still popular side-saddle. I was soon to abandon this style after returning to Pembroke and riding with Welland Williams, whose father, a lawyer, owned a small stable of good saddle horses and promised to teach me to jump fences if I would 'throw away that skirt and get a good pair of riding breeks.'

After two years at Branksome Hall I returned home with an advanced certificate in piano from the University of Toronto, and the school medal, given in my graduation year for the first time.

Suddenly I was faced with a life that seemed to have no purpose. My days in school had been happy. I had enjoyed my studies and the wonderful sense of achievement. The girls I had associated with were also keen students, several of them planning to enter university. They had the good fortune to live in Toronto, but for me there was the restricted life of a small town. There were social duties, going calling with my mother and always being careful to leave the correct number of cards. Scarcely more enjoyable were the endless ladies' tea-parties. I felt myself stagnating completely until I discovered Mr Rickwood, the organist of the Methodist church. He was a true musician with the remarkable gift of absolute pitch, and when he consented to give me lessons on the pipe-organ a rift opened in the clouds.

Ramsey and I had always been interested in reading, especially the adventure stories in the *Boy's Own Annual*, and all of the exciting tales by G.H. Henty. We had always regretted that in our peaceful world nothing exciting was ever likely to happen; certainly there would be no wars. We read the novels of Sir Walter Scott, *The Talisman* with its story of the Crusades being our favourite. It was not until I became a student at Branksome Hall that I was introduced to Dickens, the Brontë sisters, and Jane Austen, and became an admirer of Robert Browning. It was also there that I discovered the history of western Europe. (The history of Canada, as it was taught to us in high school, was completely boring because of the endless clauses of treaties and the British North America Act. It had no romance.) After leaving school I began to read widely, beginning with Thomas Carlyle's history of the French Revolution.

Various activities, such as music and teaching a Sunday School class at the Presbyterian church we attended, helped to occupy my time, but still left a great void. The study of art in some form seemed to me a necessity, and when Ramsey left to attend university I begged my father to find out if I could be accepted in the School of Architecture. My father was an engineer but he also designed various local buildings and on one occasion I had helped in his office with the layout of a small park. Professor Wright's answer to my father's letter seemed to put an end to the whole idea: 'Keep your daughter at home, Jim. This is part of the School of Practical Science, a man's college, and she would not be well received.'

At that time it was taken for granted that girls would not be interested in science and mathematics, the sterner things in life being the special province of the stronger sex. It took the experience of the Great War to change this attitude in the School of Practical Science. My request to enter this male sanctuary refused, I could only hope to make myself useful at home.

My disappointment at being refused admission to the School of Architecture was suddenly dispelled when an invitation came from my uncle in the west to visit him and his wife in the summer of 1911. Osborne Morris was a popular doctor in the Okanagan Valley of British Columbia; although he had no children, he was the proud owner of two automobiles, which were now becoming quite popular. Before my father left home early in May, it was arranged that I should go west in June, travelling part way with Ramsey who was going as far as Nipigon to join his father for the summer on a railway construction job in the north country. My diary reveals my excitement:

May 8, 1911 – Father went away to the west this afternoon. He felt so lonely going away because he is not sure how soon he will be able to get home again. This time he is going directly into the work from Superior Junction. It will take him quite a few days to get in as he has to walk about eighty miles after he reaches the end of the 'iron' as the contractors call the railway line.

May 17, 1911 – Our large brother Ramsey came home at noon today from Toronto. He does look so big and strong but a little bit tired after his hard work for his examinations. He is going to be at home for a few weeks until father sends for him to go up to construction.

May 19, 1911 – This is Basil's birthday. He is sixteen years old today. To think of our baby actually being sixteen. But he is far from looking the part of a baby. He is almost a man.

May 31, 1911 – My small brother Basil is without doubt a good-natured youngster. He left his history and other studies a few minutes ago, first to catch spiders in my room and then to fill this fountain pen for me. The poor child has to begin to study hard now, for his exams are drawing near.

June 4, 1911 – What an exciting and inspiring day this has been. This morning after church I received a telegram from Father saying to start for the west with Ramsey on Wednesday. That means two days to get ready for a three-month trip. Since then I have been rushing about getting substitutes for several things, particularly my Sunday School class. I feel lonesome to leave my six dear little boys because I will probably never teach them any more.

June 7, 1911 – So I am actually on the transcontinental train speeding away from home towards the Great West. Ramsey and I left at 5.24 and we had a large number of friends to see us off. I was frightfully lonesome just for a couple of minutes as the train pulled out and I left my dear sweet Mother standing on the platform and little Babee [Basil]. I love to have Ramsey on the train and wish he were coming all the way.

June 8, 1911 – In half an hour we should be at Nipigon and then father will be with us.

The journey to the west was an exciting adventure, particularly with Ramsey along for the first part of the trip. At Calgary I spent a few days with the Findlays, who had formerly lived in Pembroke. There I had a slight touch of homesickness but recovered. The Findlays had recently moved into a new house in the suburbs and had taken their grass lawn with them, which I found quite a novel idea. The most thrilling event of my visit was a horseback ride on the open prairies. 'Seemed very queer at first to be sitting astride the horse but it felt so safe,' I wrote in my diary on June 16. 'Such a feeling of freedom to go rushing over the broad Prairies towards the most beautiful sunset.'

June 18, 1911 – Banff, the wonderfully beautiful, with its towering mountains guarding it round about and watching like silent sentinels that no harm should come near the little town in the valley; and the river, the Bow River, is grand. Next to the mountains with their snow-bedecked summits I loved best the rapids of the Bow down further in the valley.

When I arrived at Sicamous Junction, Aunt Rosa was there to meet me. We spent the night there and reached Vernon at eleven o'clock the next morning. Uncle Osborne, looking just as I remembered him, picked us up in one of his motors.

I was now confronted with a new way of living. Everyone seemed so young and light-hearted. For one thing there was a preponderance of young men, mostly attractive Englishmen, who worked on fruit farms but seemed to have plenty of time for tennis and dancing. Next door to my uncle's extensive property was the tennis club with a number of excellent courts and usually a group of people eager for a game. There were dances every week, most often in people's houses in the lovely countryside around Vernon, and every fortnight at the country club on Long Lake. There were numerous picnics and tea-parties, which the men also attended.

June 25, 1911 – This has been a most glorious day, not a bit like Sunday though. It might have been any day in the week from the way we kept it. I am getting completely demoralized. Last Sunday rushing about Banff sight-seeing and this Sunday flying off in an automobile miles into the country for a little picnic and in the evening sitting watching people drink champagne and listening to the most terrific scandal. The fact of the matter is I did not exactly approve of the latter proceeding though the novelty of it on a Sunday evening was rather fascinating.

The merry life of Vernon was producing a change in my personality. Gone were the extreme reticence and shyness of my boarding school days. It came as a surprise to find what an asset my accomplishments were: my skill as a pianist was more appreciated than it had been in the east where it was not so rare, and it was a new experience to be a favoured partner on the dance floor and on the tennis courts.

So many young people here had become my friends. As well as the local girls there was my beautiful cousin Marion Martin from Rossland, who was spending the summer nearby with her mother and a friend. Later my childhood friend Gertrude arrived to visit her brother in Kamloops, but finding it dull accepted an invitation to stay with us in Vernon. Aunt Rosa's niece from New Westminster, Nora, also joined our party.

Life was a merry round of entertainments. There were many young men with whom I danced and played tennis, but the last thing I expected was almost to fall in love. 'August 16, 1911 – Another dance – this time a delightful house dance in the Coldstream. I enjoyed the whole dance very much, particularly the end of it when I met a nice-looking young Englishman who has a ranch up the Coldstream Valley near Lavington. His name is Mr. Williams and I like him very much. We danced three out of the last four dances.'

It was a busy time. On September 6 we got home from a trip in the country 'just in time to have dinner and dress for the B.C. Horse Dance. My friend, Mr. Williams, did not recognize me at first in the crowd, but after supper he discovered me and we had three dances in succession, sitting out one. He asked for the next also but I had it engaged. We had a dandy two-step together at the end.' The next day: 'Post festum – It was four o'clock when we got home after the dance. I have felt absolutely speechless all day. I wonder whom Williams reminds me of, both in looks and manner. I have discovered it is my teenage crush, Ambrose. Perhaps that is why he attracts me.'

At the end of September Aunt Rosa took us for a trip to the west coast. In New Westminster we stayed at Nora's home. 'September 21, 1911 – This is a day which will always be remembered in the history of Canada, the day on which the fate of reciprocity and the Laurier government will be decided and what a splendid decision! By the vote of the people of Canada reciprocity was completely overthrown and the Conservative government elected to power. What a victory for Canada and for the British!' A few days later, on the 26th, Nora's father took me to see a fishing boat that had just come in and was unloading halibut: 'I never saw such huge fish. They weigh from eighty to a hundred pounds each. They are placed into cold storage cars and sent away across the continent to supply the New York and other markets.'

September 26, 1911 – New Westminster. Wrote some cards and a letter to Mr. Lavington Williams. It was not really a letter – just a note but it looked like a big fat letter because I enclosed receipts for four cakes and icings. It did seem a queer thing to be sending to a young bachelor, but at Mrs. Denison's dance I promised to send them to him, and to make him a cake if I should be in Vernon when his dance took place. But alas! that promise I cannot keep. I hope he answers my note.

October 6, 1911 – Seattle, Washington. We reached here this morning at seven o'clock and have been going steadily all day. My first trip under the 'Stars and Stripes.' It is not so very different from our own country except that one sees the American flag flying everywhere and the ladies wear hats to the theatre and one can buy shoes for half the price and one uses gold and huge silver dollars instead of bills.

October 8, 1911 – Victoria, B.C. Back in Canada and I am writing this evening in the writing-room off the rotunda of the Empress Hotel. It is such a pretty hotel; the decorations are nearly all in green. We have two nice rooms on the second floor.

October 9, 1911 – We did not get down to breakfast this morning until rather late and spent the rest of the morning shopping. The Japanese shops were the most interesting to me. We had lunch at the hotel and directly afterwards took a glorious motor drive through the prettiest parts of the city and they are certainly very fine. We stopped at Government House and called on Mrs. Patterson and had tea with her, and she showed us through the whole mansion. The ballroom is gorgeous and made my heart ask for a dance in it.

October 10, 1911 – We left Victoria at two o'clock and I had a queer heartache leaving it. It looked so pretty in the sunshine, the harbour and the Empress Hotel and Parliament Buildings. The trip over to Vancouver was glorious.

October 12, 1911 – A letter I received this afternoon did give me a happy feeling because in it Mother said that she would try and get along without me for another month. I am beginning to feel like a selfish little pig staying away so long.

October 22, 1911 – I am without a doubt turning into a regular little heathen. Here is another Sunday gone past and I did not go to church at all just because I did not want to go. The Vancouver churches are not terribly exciting anyway. People don't seem to worry much about churches out here.

October 24, 1911 – Westminster again. Gertrude and I are gradually wending our way homeward. From Vancouver to Westminster and then to Vernon and then home. It will be great to be home again. I am beginning to long for it. Today when I reached here I found letters for me,

one from Father, one from Mother and one from Ramsey, who told me
that poor little Basil had his collarbone broken in the 'rush' at the university. Trust Basil to be always in the midst of everything!

Back in Vernon the round of dances, tea-parties, and paper-chases continued, as did the flirtation with Mr Williams. At one party 'when he came
along to us with plates of cakes and things I took a queer freak and
scarcely spoke to him. Gertrude insists that I was exceedingly fussed.' In
early November, returning from a long, cold motor drive to Lumby,
Uncle Osborne 'was in such a queer humour abusing poor Christopher
Williams and various people. He is afraid I am falling in love with Mr.
Williams. He disapproves of anything like that exceedingly.' But Mr Williams, 'with his dark sparkling eyes and pink cheeks,' continued to come
to tea.

November 24, 1911 – Tomorrow night at this time [Gertrude and I]
shall be at Sicamous on our way home. My last night in Vernon. I
wonder when I shall be in Vernon again, ever? I love it and the people
here. I believe I have more men friends here than in all the east put
together. It does seem strange to think how I dropped into this place,
met people so very different in numbers of ways, entered into the life
here, been a part of it until I feel quite at home among them all and then
as suddenly drop out again. In a few months it will all be just a series of
pictures hanging in memory's gallery, but they will be such interesting
pictures. I am convinced I shall actually gloat over some of them; the
wonderful motor drives when we sped along caring for nothing; the
beautiful blues and greens of Long Lake; the times when men said, 'Is
there *any* chance for the next dance, Miss Morris?'; the tennis – those
exciting tournament sets; the nine-mile drive to a dance just for the sake
of the man who gave it. Just now I am wondering if I shall see that man
again and there is a queer ache around my heart.

November 26, 1911 – On board C.P.R. train somewhere in the Rockies –
We have seen wonderful things today – the Rocky Mountains with their
winter garment of snow covering the peaks and clinging onto the evergreen trees making them like willow-plumes. The mountains look quite

different from what they did in June. It was lovely to watch the sunlight gradually turn the snowy peaks to gold and rose.

November 27,1911 – We're going home, we're going home, we're going home. That is what the wheels seem to be singing as they roll eastward. Miles and miles of bleak prairies – so desolate and cold with a slight covering of snow, frozen grass sticking above it; the poor shivering cattle and horses wandering over it. Tennyson's poem describes it rather well.

'The plain was grassy, wild and bare,
Wide, wild and open to the air
Which had built up everywhere
An under-roof of doleful grey.'

And then those lonesome-looking farm houses, each with a stack of straw and a miserable barn, dotted at long intervals over the plains.

December 1, 1911 – Home! At last we are at home again and everything does look so dear and familiar and cosy. Mother was at the station and so was Mrs. Booth and Aunt Ida. The train people laughed at the way we dropped our suitcases and ran to greet them.

December 3, 1911 – I was so happy this morning and not feeling the least bit solemn. I had a wild desire to rush around the church and embrace every man, woman and child, even to the dignified Mr. Knox standing so sedately behind the pulpit. Father came home this morning and that's partly the reason for my happiness.

December 15, 1911 – Perhaps Ramsey and Basil will be home a week from tonight – a week from tomorrow anyway. Oh! but it will be heavenly to see them, the darlings. I am crazy mad to see them both and I hope we shall be able to give them a jolly good time in the holidays.

Our hopes for the holidays did not materialize. Ramsey arrived home with bronchitis, having been sent two days early by his doctor who also was afraid that he might be in the process of developing typhoid fever. He was ill for quite a long time and did not return to university for the spring term, thus losing his year. Basil, who was now quite grown up, returned alone. He missed Ramsey, for they were accustomed to sharing a suite in East House, one of the university residences.

It was a great pleasure for me to have Ramsey at home and as he grew stronger we enjoyed doing things together, reading, skating at the rink, and snow-shoeing. A social club, which Gertrude and I had organized after we returned from British Columbia, was now the centre of our social life, with small house dances, card parties, sleigh-drives, and, towards spring when the snow was deep, snow-shoe tramps across the fields.

That spring the outside intruded only slightly upon our quiet world.

April 16, 1912 – People can talk of nothing today but that frightful disaster, the wreck of the great new ship, the Titanic, in her first voyage. At first the papers said that all the people on board had been saved but later reports say that of 2,200 people, which the vessel carried, only eight hundred and some were rescued, picked up from lifeboats by another ship, the Carpathian. All the others went down with the Titanic, down to the uttermost depths of the ocean – two miles it is said. It is really too awful to think about and beyond one's powers to realize. I can remember distinctly seeing a moving picture show in Vancouver last October, a picture of the launching of the Titanic, the largest vessel ever built, and now it lies at the bottom of the ocean with its thirteen hundred victims and a valuable cargo of diamonds and mail.

That winter I was asked to replace the art teacher at Pembroke High School. I was amazed, almost flabbergasted, by the request, for it seemed such a short time since I had been there as a student. On my first day I was so frantically nervous at noon that I could not eat any lunch. But the classes were orderly and I gradually gained confidence. As the course required some perspective drawing I persuaded my father to teach me something about it one evening. I also tried to give my pupils an idea of composition, the placing of their drawings on the paper, and a few useful rules. The whole course was rather vague and for the first form it was not of great importance, but for form II it required a regular examination for the girls who would be entering model school to be trained as teachers.

As soon as my art classes were finished in the spring of 1912, I went to Toronto to attend a Branksome Hall reunion. I was made vice-president of the Alumnae Association, the only office given to someone living outside the city. Following a visit with my former roommate Lorraine to her parents' cottage on Lake of Bays, I returned to spend the summer in Pembroke with my mother, as she would be alone.

Ramsey, just turned nineteen, had decided to spend some time away from home and hoped to find a job for a couple of months in Calgary. He succeeded in being hired as a teamster on a construction project, but as he knew nothing about horses this soon came to an end. He was then offered a job teaching at a small school on the prairies close to the American border; being a university student seemed to be all that was required as qualification. To his surprise his pupils, recently arrived from the United States, asked him for a holiday to celebrate their national day, the Fourth of July. He solved the problem by agreeing to their request, provided they would also take a holiday on the First of July to celebrate Canada's national day. They were pleased with the arrangement. When he found that the children would be well supplied with Stars and Stripes for the picnic on the Fourth, he quickly sent home for as many Union Jacks as could be located. Soon a large bundle was on its way. The students enjoyed both events, but the most important result was that they learned they were now Canadians. At the end of his assignment Ramsey paid a short visit to Uncle Osborne in the Okanagan Valley.

At this time my father was occupied with a contract to build a section of the new transcontinental railway in northern Ontario. Having left his engineering practice in Pembroke in the hands of his junior partner, he spent much of his time in the northern wilderness. The only way to reach his work, at the divisional point which is now the town of Armstrong, was by walking ninety miles along the right of way from Fort William on Lake Superior. In the summer of 1912, feeling that Basil was now old enough to learn some of the practical aspects of his future profession of engineering, he took him into the north with him. They left about the middle of May, when the black flies were at their worst, and camped at intervals along the way, taking several days to reach their destination. Basil's job was to be timekeeper, which required him to keep the score of all the hours of work done by the labourers, most of whom were Finnish and excellent workmen according to my father. With a permanent camp and storehouses for all their supplies, life was fairly comfortable. A carload of canned tomatoes took the place of fresh fruit. One night disaster struck when a forest fire destroyed most of their storehouses; it was also a financial disaster as it had been impossible to insure buildings in the forest. Basil returned from his summer's work sturdier and taller and ready for his second year at the School of Practical Science.

My own life was made more interesting by visits to Ottawa, where I often stayed with my cousins the McDougalls, to me a large and fascinating family. One attraction in Ottawa was the splendid Russell Theatre, where one could see fine productions from New York of plays and musical shows such as *The Red Rose* and *The Pink Lady*. We enjoyed dancing to the music of these productions, especially the romantic waltz song 'To You, Beautiful Lady, I Raise My Eyes.' With a good partner, one felt transported into a world of pure romance.

The State Ball at Rideau Hall had all the quality of a magnificent pageant. Our member of Parliament and his wife took me as their guest, and we stayed at the new Chateau Laurier. I was interviewed by a newspaper reporter who came to get a description of my dress; this I found quite amusing, but it was indeed a lovely dress of peach-coloured satin with diamanté trimming.

November 27, 1912 – The ball was magnificent – a beautiful sight but not exactly the place to have fun. There were crowds and crowds of people, all packed into the ballroom; ladies in gorgeous dresses and most of the men in uniforms; military in scarlet tunics and the cabinet ministers in Windsor uniforms of green and gold. A space was left leading to the thrones when the Governor-General's party entered! First the aides, then the Duke and Duchess, followed by Princess Patricia and then the ladies-in-waiting. The lancers of honour were formed and danced, the Duke with Mrs. Borden and the Duchess with Mr. Borden; it seemed a very solemn proceeding. Then the other dancing started, everyone bumping into everyone else. I had a few dances with some old MP's.

As we walked through a long corridor when leaving, I noticed a distinguished-looking man standing alone. My escort said 'That is Sir Wilfrid Laurier. A few months ago, he would not be standing alone.'

In spite of the fun and excitement of my social life my father realized that there was something missing, and he suggested that I should go to his office sometimes when he was there and try engineering draughting, copying plans. He was pleased with my efforts and one day had me sign a document, an agreement to be his apprentice in architecture.

All the time, however, I had dreams of some day becoming an artist.

August 19, 1912 – While the others played bridge, I sat in the hammock and watched the wonderful play of sunlight and shadow on the lawn and among the trees. There is a great fascination about sunlight and shade. It seems to take one's mind wandering away off into fairyland, and makes it revel in daydreams. Sometimes fairyland consists of reveries of a dear little town nestling among dream hills in a sunny Okanagan Valley, and kind-hearted, jolly people there, one with dark sparkling eyes, and sometimes the dream castles are built of landscape sketches in oils and watercolours with a name attached which has won fame, and music which wins the hearts of people, and knowledge of many things and perhaps ... but this is absolute nonsense I am writing.

September 15, 1912 – The book I am reading is the story of a woman's search for knowledge of life – to know the real meaning of living and all it has to give. A colourless life with no great joys or sorrows is the saddest of all.

October 3, 1912 – When the real autumn days come, there is not anything more beautiful in the whole year. My great longing is to paint some of the beauty – put it down on canvas where I shall always have it. I went out to the pasture where Father and I walked yesterday and sat myself down upon a stone. Unfortunately just as I started, the sun went behind a cloud and stayed there for the remainder of the afternoon.

October 4, 1912 – After lunch about half-past one I packed up my paint-box and brushes and sketching things and started out to the fields. There were ever so many cows in the pasture, some rather fierce-looking, but I found a large pile of logs, which formed a most comfortable seat, safe out of reach of my bovine enemies and commanding an excellent view of the pasture and a group of beautiful birch and oak trees. I painted very industriously and got so interested in my subject that everything was forgotten until the sunlight began to fade from the fields and I realized that evening had come; but it was a glorious afternoon and I feel quite proud of my little sketch.

October 5, 1912 – The marvelous beauty of these autumn days are beyond any ordinary human being's powers to describe – the glory of them – the harvest fields and beside them the woods all shimmering gold and red, and the mysterious violet haze shrouding the distant trees and hills. It is all like a wonderful dream of perfect beauty – it almost chokes me. Oh! if I could only paint it! Even if the picture fails utterly I think that it is worth while to go out into the fields and worship the beauty and the Divine Artist who created it.

Increasingly, my time was occupied by music. Singing lessons were developing my voice with some success so that I became a soloist in the church choir and sometimes sang at concerts. A choral society was formed in Pembroke in which I participated.

Another winter passed. Ramsey and Basil roomed together again at East House. In the summer of 1913 Ramsey went north to work on construction and Basil joined a survey party in Algonquin Park as part of his engineering training. The highlight of my summer was a two-week-long house party at Lorraine's cottage on Lake of Bays in the Muskoka country north of Toronto. Among the young crowd there were two of my favourite people, Ambrose Moffat and his sister Mary, old friends from Toronto who had often visited their aunt in Pembroke.

Ambrose and I spent many happy hours together, playing tennis, drifting in canoes on the winding Oxtongue River, discussing history, poetry, and many things. One afternoon at teatime he caused great merriment by complaining to the assembled company that I would never let him kiss me.

We were young, and like young people of all generations we loved to dance. New styles in dancing, invented by Vernon Castle and his wife in England, were finally reaching Pembroke; Irene Castle not only helped to create the new rhythms but also introduced the fashion for women of bobbing their hair.

Everywhere people were dancing a new one-step to a tune called 'Très moutard,' as well as the tango and a new version of the waltz known as the 'hesitation waltz.' A dancing master arrived in Pembroke, taught us the steps, and by Christmas, when the boys came home for their holidays, the craze had caught on.

The 'thé dansant' had become a favourite form of entertainment. Held at the tea-hour, five o'clock in the afternoon, it generally lasted for two hours or more, the dancers scarcely stopping to sip their tea.

On the afternoon of New Year's Day 1914, Ramsey, Basil, and I entertained our friends, many of whom were home for the Christmas holidays. We danced in the large living room and tea was served in the dining room. How difficult to explain to our aunt, waiting to entertain the family at New Year's dinner, that we were late because we could hardly persuade our guests to stop dancing.

2 ❋ Alf's story ❋ ❋ ❋ ❋ ❋ ❋ ❋ ❋ ❋

July 1914, a perfect month for a vacation. The sun was shining and the world was at peace, as it had been for so long that the thought of war, if anyone thought about it at all, was something that belonged to past generations.

Both my brothers were home in Pembroke for what they considered to be well-earned holidays, having successfully completed their year's work at the University of Toronto.

Ramsey, at twenty, had just finished his third year in political science, having lost a year at university because of illness. He hoped to get his Bachelor of Arts degree the following year, and then enter Osgoode Hall to study law. He was a serious, studious young man, fond of reading and arguing. Tall and handsome, he had a humorous twinkle in his dark eyes, and brown hair that insisted on curling in spite of his constant efforts to prevent it.

Basil was quite different. Of medium height, he had unruly auburn hair and a happy smile. He won hearts easily and seemed to enjoy every aspect of his life. He was always laughing. Now eighteen, he had one more year of study to complete before receiving his degree in civil engineering at the School of Practical Science; thereafter he planned to join his father's firm. His favourite expression, as recorded in the *Torontonensis*, was 'Oh, why should life all labour be.' With his penchant for fun and his sense that life was to be enjoyed, he was not a scholar and never stood at the top of his class, but he made decent grades and always seemed to be a year younger than anyone else in his classes.

Both boys were popular with the girls of their age group, but neither as yet had lost his heart.

Basil's engineering course required him to spend several weeks each summer with a survey party and he was working in Algonquin Park at the beginning of July when Ramsey's friend and classmate Alf Bastedo arrived in Pembroke to stay with us for a month. The visit had been planned when my mother and I were in Toronto early in the spring.

Alf was an attractive young man, of medium height and slight of build, with a quick athletic response in all his movements. He played an excellent game of tennis and had just won his 'T' as a champion tennis player at the university. Ramsey counted on me to help entertain his friend. On his first morning at our place I took him to the tennis club for a friendly, chatty game. When, to his chagrin, he found that I had taken the set, he vowed that it would never happen again, and it never did.

Since this was Alf's first visit to the Upper Ottawa Valley we planned that he should see and enjoy all the places we loved; we felt sure that he would appreciate the history as well as the beauty of the area.

Our first picnic was on Morrison's Island, in the Ottawa River a few miles below the town. The island had been described by Champlain in his diary as 'an impregnable fortress,' being protected on two sides by fast-flowing rapids. The still water at the upper end of the island provided the safest approach and here we beached our canoes. Following a rocky path along the southern rapids, called the Lost Cheneil, we arrived at a sandy beach where the village of the Algonquin chief Tasouat had stood. Champlain had visited there in 1613 and nearby, on the mainland, he had lost his astrolabe. It was still possible to find Indian arrowheads in the area.

Another day, perhaps the most exciting of all, we went on a picnic at Oiseau Rock, upriver beyond our cottage at Fort William, where the river turns sharply west and flows through a great trench at the base of the Laurentian Mountains. Once upon a time the rock, rising hundreds of feet above the water in a sheer cliff, had been held sacred by the Indians, and from it they offered gifts to the Great Spirit. From a cove near the base we climbed a steep, rocky path leading to the top, where we suddenly came upon a beautiful lake surrounded by hills. White water-lilies floated on the dark water and black water snakes, disturbed by our voices, slithered off rocks and rotting logs and disappeared into the depths. From the edge of the cliff, which we approached with great care, the forest seemed to stretch endlessly; far below the solemn river moved quietly past the headlands. We had our picnic near the shore and danced on the wooden wharf to the music of a squeaky gramophone while waiting for the steamer to return.

During our trips on the river that summer we were sometimes aware of a new sound – a sound, as we later learned, that meant more to Alf than to the rest of us. Ten miles west of Pembroke, at Petawawa, an artillery camp had been established a few years earlier. It stretched from the Petawawa River along the south shore of the Ottawa to Chalk River. The great sandy plain was ideal for the manoeuvring of guns and vehicles and, since the camp extended for many miles back into the wilderness, it was also ideal for the practice of long-range firing. To the people who lived here the distant boom of the guns had already become a familiar sound, and if they noticed them as they travelled along the river they would remark casually: 'The guns are firing today.'

Guns? Why guns?

As the happy days of this lovely summer slipped by, no one really noticed the dark clouds that had appeared on the horizon. We scarcely heeded the message in the news that the heir to the Austrian throne had been assassinated at a place called Sarajevo in the distant Balkans. There had been rumours of war in eastern Europe, but it all seemed very far away. Nor did we pay much attention to the vastly expanded German navy or the blustery slogan 'Deutschland über Alles.' The Kaiser seemed to us a sinister figure, ambitious, but no immediate threat. In Canada we had been brought up to realize our good fortune in being part of the British Empire, shown coloured pink in great areas on the world map, and we felt we would be safe anywhere, protected by a navy that ruled the seas. It was a comfortable, secure feeling.

But now it was apparent to all that Germany had plans for acquiring a world empire of its own. News came that the Kaiser's troops had invaded Belgium on their way to France, and Britain was threatening to declare war.

On August 4, 1914, we sat tensely on the verandah of our home in Pembroke, Ramsey, Alf, our cousin Sammie, and myself. We were waiting for Basil, the youngest of the group, to return from the telegraph office where he had been sent to read the latest bulletin. Could our country possibly be in danger?

As Basil hurried up the steps he announced breathlessly: 'War is declared. Canada is at war!' Silence. Then someone said: 'But this is *our* war! How do you get into a war?' 'I know how I get into it,' Alf replied. 'I leave on the early morning train for home. I am a captain in the militia in Milton.'

We wondered how long a war could last in this industrial age. A few weeks, possibly? There might be fighting at sea, but if Canadians were to defend Canada where would the battle line be? Not likely on this continent – more probably in Europe where the war had begun.

The next morning we went to the railway station to bid farewell to Alf. In a little while a letter came from him saying that he was at Valcartier, a military camp which had been set up about twenty miles northwest of Quebec City. Here the first Canadian contingent was being assembled and organized for service overseas. By early September over thirty thousand volunteers had arrived. At the beginning of October, men, horses, and equipment sailed down the St Lawrence in a great armada, gathered into a convoy at Gaspé, and under Royal Navy escort sailed across the Atlantic to England. To most Canadians, especially those of British descent, it was a proud moment, for we were now taking part in the defence of the Empire.

When we heard from Alf again he was with the 1st Canadian Division encamped on Salisbury Plain in the south of England. There the Canadian soldiers spent the winter months under canvas in almost continuous rain. Their training completed, they crossed the English Channel in the spring of 1915 and took up their position in the salient protecting the important Belgian city of Ypres. In April Alf sent me the following letter.

4th Bn. Canadian Expeditionary Force

Dear Grace,

I had a letter from your father a day or two ago and was very pleased to hear from him. I have been enjoying life rather well of late, haven't been working too hard but expect to get into it a bit harder before long.

One sees some rather dreadful sights in this place which it pays to forget about as quickly as possible and not to write about at all, so I try to remember only the nice things. I was in England last week in charge of a bunch of men returning to Canada. I had the opportunity of going over with them with 10 days leave on the other side but refused it and some other fellow went. Now I am on my way to the front again.

I guess we won't have much tennis this year. By the way, I'm getting to be quite a French linguist. I manage to make out most of what is said to me and get them to understand. I hope to be quite efficient before long and then when I see you again, I'll be quite too much for you. I would be very glad to hear from you if you would be so kind.

Yours, Alf

The Second Battle of Ypres began early in the morning of April 22, 1915. The soldiers of the 1st Canadian Division, in their first large-scale action of the war, were holding a section of the Allied line defending Ypres; next to them, on the left, was a French division of colonial troops. Suddenly the men were amazed to see in front of them a cloud of whitish vapour gradually turning to greenish-brown and yellow; impelled by a northern breeze, it was crossing the space between the trenches towards them. Beside a huge gap in the line left by the dying or fleeing French colonials, the Canadians held firm, though their trenches too were soon filled with the choking gas. In this, their first battle, they had proven themselves superb soldiers and had frustrated a vital German push on the Western Front. The news of their heroic stand was received with great pride, and Canadians realized that their country, until now little known, had decisively stepped onto the world stage.

Then came the first casualty list. Beneath a banner headline, 'Canada Forever and Forever,' were the names of the gallant men who had fallen in battle. In Pembroke the long list was posted in the window of the telegraph office on Main Street. People stood in the street to read it. There was silence and deep sorrow.

At the top of the list was the name 'Captain Alfred Bastedo – killed in action.'

3 ❈ The crossing ❈❈❈❈❈❈❈❈

When Alf Bastedo left Pembroke in August 1914 to join his regiment in Milton, Ramsey and Basil had already discussed the matter of enlistment with their father. Both wanted to join the overseas army at once. Although sympathetic to his sons' eagerness, his advice was both practical, in terms of the family's well-being, and ironical, as things turned out: as the eldest son, he said, Ramsey should have the privilege of going overseas first; Basil should return to university to complete his course in engineering.

Thus Ramsey left immediately for the military camp at Valcartier, hoping to join the first Canadian contingent to be sent abroad. An intelligent recruiting officer there, realizing that many young officers would be required for the Canadian expeditionary force, persuaded him to return home in order to apply for a commission and get training as an officer. Ramsey accepted this advice, returned to Pembroke, and applied for his commission in the 42nd Lanark and Renfrew Regiment. When this was granted, he was accepted in the 38th Battalion, then being organized in Ottawa, and sent for training to Barriefield camp near Kingston.

Not to be left out of things, Basil also applied for and was granted a commission in the same regiment. Thus when he returned to university and joined the Canadian Officers Training Corps under Lieutenant Colonel H.H. Madill, he was one of the few commissioned officers in that organization.

Despite the rigour of his studies, the young officer was able to play an active role in the war. In a discussion of recruiting and unemployment in *Ontario and the First World War, 1914-1918*, Barbara Wilson described one of his activities: 'One rural regiment, the 42nd Lanark and Renfrew, took advantage of the unemployment situation to reach their quota for the CEF. The *Globe* reported on 17 February [1915] that Lieut. B.M. Morris had persuaded 133 men from rural areas who were unemployed and living in Toronto to return with him to Smiths Falls to enlist. Toronto's Civic Employment Bureau had 133 fewer jobs to find.' The incident was typical of Basil's enthusiasm.

When his university year was completed in the spring of 1915, Basil went with the COTC to a camp at Niagara to complete his training as an officer. He then joined the 59th Battalion at Barriefield, and shortly thereafter was appointed machine-gun officer.

Towards the end of 1915, when the war in Europe seemed to be at a standstill, a group of smartly uniformed officers appeared in Pembroke. They were an advance party for the First Canadian Tunnelling Company which was beginning to assemble in the town armouries. The unit was being hastily organized by the Department of Militia and Defence for service in France in hopes of helping to end the stalemate in trench warfare by means of mining under the lines. While the officers were mainly professional mining engineers, the men for the most part were hard-rock miners recruited in northern Ontario and the Maritimes; miners were also drafted from battalions already organized. Pembroke, with its large, empty armouries that could be used as headquarters, seemed a sensible, central location in which to mobilize. The soldiers were received with warm hospitality by the people of the town, particularly the local girls, who were delighted to find so many fine-looking young men in uniform on the streets.

The Officer Commanding the unit, Major R.P. Rogers, had been manager of the Coniagas Mine in Cobalt; he was pleased to find that he had known the mayor of the town, my father, for a number of years through a professional engineers' organization, and with his co-operation a large old house was acquired as an officers' mess.

Our house, located not far from the mess, soon had the aspect of an annex. When the OC's attractive young wife announced that she would journey from Cobalt to visit her husband, he discovered that the accommodation offered by the local hotels left much to be desired. The problem was solved when my mother invited the visitor to be our guest. Thus Mary Rogers became the first wartime addition to our household.

When Major Rogers learned that his friend's young son Basil was a recent graduate in engineering and a machine-gun officer in training at

Barriefield, he asked for his transfer to the Tunnellers; although the company had many clever engineers, it was short of officers with military training. To our delight, Basil returned to Pembroke in early December 1915.

Other young people arrived in town. One day the adjutant, Captain Bill May, returned from weekend leave in Montreal with a pretty bride: Winnifred Weir, the daughter of Judge Robert Stanley Weir, who had written the most commonly sung English version of 'O Canada.' The Mays, as well as other young officers, often came over for social evenings to meet my family and friends.

One November evening a telephone call suddenly interrupted one of these gatherings. The agitated voice of the town policeman shouted: 'Come quickly! Your men are rioting on the main street outside the office of the *Deutsche Post*. They are yelling for the editor and threaten to pull the presses into the street.'

Within a few minutes the rioting soldiers were confronted by their officers, who soon found the reason for the turmoil: the *Post*, which was still being published in German, had foolishly printed an editorial in defence of the sinking of the *Lusitania* and the rioters were demanding a retraction. With all possible speed the editor of the paper had rushed down to his office where he had been confronted by an angry mob. He was ordered to write an apology, have it printed in English, and posted in the armouries by morning. Wisely he did as he was told and the *Deutsche Post* was never again printed in German.

Just before Christmas the company suddenly had orders to get ready to entrain for overseas service. A farewell dance for the officers was held in the town hall. Among these officers was Stuart Thorne, who had come from Cobalt where he had been manager of the Trethewey Mine. He was a friend of my cousin in Ottawa and had brought an introduction from her. With his rugged, strong good looks and droll humour, he was a delightful companion, and I felt flattered when he invited me to be his partner for the dance. He danced well and we enjoyed ourselves. I had an impression of the strength of this man as I danced with my face close to the polished leather of the officers' Sam Brown belt over his shoulder, with its masculine army smell. The firmness with which he held me gave me a feeling of security, knowing that soldiers like this were going to defend us. I wondered if he would ever think of me after he left and hoped that he would.

On the day of their departure, December 30, 1915, the men of the company marched from the armouries to the station opposite the post office where a crowd of townspeople had gathered to wish them well. There was much confusion but finally they were all aboard, and the officers took their places in the drawing-room car. With them were three smartly dressed young women carrying overnight bags, casually sitting in comfortable chairs and chatting with the men. In a few minutes a train-dispatcher rushed in and breathlessly announced: 'Ladies, this train is leaving in two minutes.' Nobody moved. The feeling of tension dissolved into merriment as the train pulled away. The OC was nowhere to be seen.

As regulations required that a military unit must have all its nominal rolls, medical history sheets, and other documents in order before it could leave Canada, there was no time to lose. The drawing-room car was quickly turned into a busy office. Mary Rogers, who could type, was put at a typewriter, while Winnifred May and I were assigned minor jobs. We had to earn our transportation before reaching Ottawa, three hours away, where undoubtedly the joke would come to an end when the Defence Department inspected the train.

Up to our ears in piles of paper when we arrived in the capital, we hardly noticed the long wait while a new section was added to the train to accommodate a detachment of engineers on their way to France as reinforcements. These were trained troops and they looked askance at the casual style of the miners; in the officers' car, for instance, several had changed their heavy army boots for carpet slippers to be more comfortable while they did their office work.

All this time the OC remained mysteriously absent. When Major Rogers finally returned there was a twinkle in his eyes as he announced that the First Canadian Tunnelling Company could now proceed overseas; he had been to Defence headquarters and had arranged that three supernumeraries should be officially added to the company to help complete its documents before reaching the port of embarkation.

All the next day, as the train rolled along, work proceeded without interruption until evening, when Basil, who had been assigned the duty of officer of the day, reported that there was trouble in the men's cars. There was much grumbling and threat of a revolt. The men, in need of exercise and wishing to let off steam, were demanding to be taken on a route march through Moncton, where the train was stopped for an hour. The engineers' officers had taken their men on such an expedition, but the Tunnellers' CO felt that he could not risk losing part of his company if the tough, hard-rock miners happened to fancy a pub instead of a troop train; it was New Year's Day and they had been subjected to very little military discipline.

It was then that Mary, Win, and I helped to ease the situation. We remembered that a great many cartons of cigarettes had been given to the officers by their friends in Pembroke. Basil especially had a large supply, for many friends in his home town had said farewell to him at the station. Cheerfully he handed over his treasure trove. We then visited the dining-car to borrow trays, and there the steward co-operated by donating biscuits and any sweets he had available.

With all the self-confidence we could muster we entered the long cars. Some of the men were wandering about in an aimless fashion, but mostly they were lying quietly in their bunks reading. At the appearance of three young women the atmosphere changed rapidly. As we walked down the long aisles distributing our small gifts and best wishes for the New Year, shaking hands and exchanging jokes, the sullen mood vanished and laughter took its place.

Late that evening the train slipped quietly onto a dock in Saint John, where a great, grim troopship, the converted CPR liner *R.M.S. Metagama*, stood waiting. The men were quickly marched aboard.

The three of us, lonely women, stood beside the sheds and watched the ship disappear into the murk. The government official in charge of the train then escorted us to our hotel in the middle of the city.

In Saint John it was cold and gloomy. The wind blew in from the sea and snow fell on the empty streets.

A few days later I wrote to Basil abroad for the first time.

Jan. 3, 1916

Dear Babee,

We are still in St. John, but expect to leave this evening on the I.C.R. about six o'clock. When your great dark boat moved out and sailed away it was very lonesome, but we watched the lights until they were almost out of sight, and they did indeed go quickly ...

Mrs. Rogers, Mrs. May and I went with Captain Watson to a very nice café and had supper. That was a very queer party! Imagine, Babee, four people, who a month ago had not even known of the existence of one another, having supper together at midnight in a strange city, and so tired that it mattered not what they were offered for food. It is marvelous that we are living to tell the tale after consuming oysters and then lobster salad ...

There was a recruiting meeting in the Imperial theatre last night, and when we heard that Father Burke of Toronto was to speak at it, we thought it worthwhile to go. There were throngs at it and we were ushered up to seats in the orchestra stalls almost under the stage. The whole meeting lasted just three-quarters of an hour, but it was very impressive, and the great wonder is how hundreds of young men in 'civies' could sit quietly and listen to Father Burke speak. It made me almost want to disappear under the stage just because I was not a man in khaki ...

When I go home perhaps I shall write a story of that queer trip on the troop train for you and Mr. Jeffrey and Mr. Thorne. It was their parting request from the boat and must be complied with. With best regards to all 'the Tunnellers' ...

Your sister,
Grace Morris

It has taken me over sixty-five years to fulfil that request, made to me in the darkness of Saint John harbour in the evening hours of New Year's Day, 1916.

Meanwhile Basil had written his first letter home, and on the ship, as he had promised, he kept a diary, which he sent home to us in a letter. A young soldier finally on his way to war, he was full of the sense of adventure.

Atlantic Ocean
R.M.S. Metagama
January 2nd/16

Dear Mother and Father,

This is the most interesting experience I have ever had in my life and I am enjoying it to the full. As I said before, this is the best part of the war.

Last night we pulled out at 10:30 p.m. I said good-bye to Grace and the others and came on board and went up on deck. Two tugs, one at the bow and the other at the stern, pulled us away from the wharf and headed us down stream. The last I saw of Grace and the others was under the light on the dock as we went out of sight and they gradually disappeared. I can hardly realize even yet that I am on my way to the front at last but I am now on my second stage of the journey. This boat is a very fine one. The men are steerage, most of the officers are 2nd and the senior officers have 1st class. The meals are very good indeed. At our table in the dining room there are about 30. I know an awful bunch of chaps on this boat which is fine as it makes it very nice.

Jan. 2nd – I did not get up till 8:30 this morning and had a most beautiful sleep. These bunks surely are comfortable.

Jan. 3rd – This is my second morning on the ocean and I have got pretty well used to it. The time passes very quickly. We are having a snowstorm and it is terribly cold outside. The decks are so crowded that there is no room to drill much, but we have to practice falling in with our lifebelts on at the alarm post which in our case is the forward deck.

Jan. 4th – We are another day farther on our course towards England. The storm is over but the boat is rolling quite a bit still. It is wonderful to stand in the bow and watch the waves come from away on the horizon and gradually approach. There are quite a few sick this morning among our officers. I am hoping for the best. We had a morning parade this morning and life-belt drill. Every morning at breakfast we get the latest news Marconi but I cannot say that it is terribly cheerful to hear about such a boat being torpedoed. We will likely pick up our escort in a day or two now.

Jan. 5th – We expect to land on Monday but there is no telling as we are making very slow time on account of the headwind, and are on a longer route than ordinarily would be taken. I would not miss this trip for worlds and after the war is over am going to take this trip for pleasure.

Jan. 6th – We are about half way across now and I am having a wonderful time. It is like summer almost and the sea is very calm.
  The nurses on board are not a pretty bunch by any means when compared to others on shore but now since we have seen no other women

for nearly a week, are getting to be quite good-looking it seems. I suppose before we are through this war we will think them queens.

Jan. 7th – We are evidently nearing England. There is nothing very exciting happening. I was up on the hurricane deck for a couple of hours last night with Billy May and it was wonderful up there with a clear sky overhead and the stars shining brightly.

We had a medical inspection today.

Jan. 8th – Just a week ago today I left Canada and said good-bye to Grace. The picture of the wharf and Grace, Mrs. Rogers, Capt. Watson and Mrs. May under the light by the door of the shed will never be blotted out of my mind as it was impressed pretty well on me. It was the last sight I had of Canada and I surely will remember it. I was mighty glad that Grace came down on the troop train with us as she worked hard and it was great to have her there.

Jan. 9th – Today we have orders to go around carrying our life-preservers wherever we go. All the windows were blanketed last night and no lights shown whatever. We could not even strike a match on deck. We have not picked up our escort but have run across a number of large boats and trawlers. All the life-boats are swung out, the rope ladders in position and the gun on our stern all ready for use.

The officers have to carry loaded revolvers around in case of anything happening. The men might try to rush the boats. It is quite an awesome feeling to feel a revolver in my pocket and to realize that it is there in earnest.

12:10 p.m. the torpedo boat destroyers have just come up, they are wonderful little boats and we feel a whole lot safer.

Jan. 12th – We landed at Plymouth on Monday morning. It was wonderful stealing along through the night without a light showing anywhere, and we could not distinguish the destroyers who were escorting us. It was quite an odd experience.

Basil

Grace Morris

On the trip out west in 1911: Banff (left); Uncle Osborne's car in Vernon; Grace and Gertrude on the steps of the Empress Hotel in Victoria

A survey party in Algonquin Park, summer 1914; Basil is in the centre

Dancing on the dock at Oiseau Rock

Left Going up the Ottawa on the *S.S. Oiseau*; Alf Bastedo is smoking a pipe

Last leave together at home in Pembroke: Ramsey, Grace, Basil

Ramsey at Barriefield camp

Basil and Marie at Oiseau Rock

Welland Williams
on board the *Missanabie*

The *Metagama*, on which Basil crossed the Atlantic

Officers of the No 1 Canadian Tunnelling Company on arrival in England:
Basil and Bob Murray on the right, back row; Stuart Thorne on the left,
front row, with Major R.P. Rogers in the centre, the adjutant Bill May on his left

4 ❋ Up the line ❋ ❋ ❋ ❋ ❋ ❋ ❋ ❋ ❋

The Tunnellers did not stay long in England. After a brief spell at a camp in Buckinghamshire, they entrained for Southampton where they embarked upon the transport *Manchester Importer*, arriving in Le Havre on February 16, 1916. They had had little real military training before entering upon active service, since they had come for a specific purpose – mining.

Early in March they were moved up to the Armentières front to take over the mining operations from a company of Royal Engineers. Then, in May, under a new commander, Major C.B. North, they were moved on to La Clytte and then put in charge of offensive mining at St Eloi on the south side of the Ypres salient. This section of the front was held for years mainly by Canadian troops against strong enemy pressure; situated along the border between France and Belgium, the line of the trenches shifted back and forth through the two countries. Since Basil was not allowed to reveal his exact position in his letters, it was impossible to know precisely where he was located on the line.

Tunnelling was particularly difficult in this section because the soil consisted largely of clay and quicksand rather than the usual chalk. In general the miners' job was to sink shafts and extend tunnels under 'no man's land' towards the enemy trenches. Through the mud and water of the galleries they crawled, like human moles, quietly listening for the enemy. Their work was both offensive and defensive, a matter of mining and counter-mining: they endeavoured to blow up the German trenches from below and at the same time to prevent the Germans in their tunnels from reaching the Allied defensive positions. Long lengths of tunnel were therefore driven not only with the intention of destroying the enemy's works but also with the object of locating, by means of listening devices, the existence of enemy tunnellers. Sometimes hand-to-hand combat took place underground, with those on the surface being unaware of what was happening below. For large operations, mines were prepared well in advance and not blown until the final big moment.

Flooding was one of the greatest hazards, for water sometimes filled the galleries and had to be pumped out. There was the danger, too, of poison gas being released in the tunnels by the enemy. The miners carried cages of canaries to give warning of gas, for if the birds keeled over they knew it was time to get out, if they could. Always there was the misery of mud.

The Tunnellers shared the trenches with the infantry battalion on duty. As Basil explained in one of his letters, they therefore ran the same risks in their dugouts from enemy fire but at least they were not required to 'go over the top.' The men in the infantry, for their part, were usually horrified by the thought of fighting underground, deep in the mud they had come to loathe. But the miners, used to the idea of being underground anyway, felt safer away from the bursting shells and machine-gun fire on the surface.

The work of the Tunnellers was highly secret and could not be discussed even with the infantry officers in the same trenches. In one letter, however, Basil inadvertently disclosed the depth to which they sometimes mined when he noted that a large prehistoric bone had been found some forty feet below the trenches.

Censorship played an important part in the amount of information a soldier could enclose in his letters from the front: nothing that in any way gave aid or comfort to the enemy must ever be mentioned, because even letters sent home to one's family might fall into the wrong hands. Therefore, few details of the misery they endured, the horrors of trench warfare, or the work they were doing appear in the letters. An officer, such as Basil, censored the letters of the men under his command; his own letters were self-censored.

Basil's early letters from France showed a slight dampening of his youthful enthusiasm as he came to realize that fighting on the Western Front was 'going to be no picnic,' as he put it. There was a long and tough job ahead. But he was enjoying himself, observing his new surroundings, and pleased to find he could use his high school French. His main concern seemed to be that his family would worry about him. Being younger than the other officers, most of whom were professional mining engineers, he was also concerned about his lack of experience, for he had never been down a mineshaft before he reached the trenches.

Feb. 15th 1916

My Dear Mother,

We are now in France. I am very sorry that I cannot tell you when or where we landed or where we are now, but we are not yet in the firing line.

On coming over we had a brute of a trip across the channel. I can quite believe any stories I have heard of the English Channel. We disembarked in the pouring rain and had to march quite a piece in a regular deluge. The men are in tents and we are also, but there is a comfortable officer's mess here.

The French soldiers are most damnably sloppy-looking and their blue uniforms are quite funny. We saw a batch of German prisoners on our march up and they were a pretty husky-looking lot. I do not feel as excited as I had expected I would be on coming to the front.

Please do not worry over me because if I am going to get mine, it cannot be avoided and your worrying will not help matters at all. Just hope for the best and trust that I will come back safely.

The officers' mail is not censored but we just put our name on the envelope which is our guarantee that no names of places, units etc. are mentioned in our letters at all.

Lots of love again, Mother, and please do not worry as the thought of you worrying over me is worse than the thought of the trenches.

I would like very much to go to a regular church service once before I go to the firing line. I have not been to one since I left home. I surely hope that this old war will be over soon as I can see from our trip so far that this is going to be no picnic but hard plugging and needs lots of patience and a good nerve.

Your loving son, Basil

France, 17/2/16

Dear Father,

I have just been answering letters for the last half hour. I wish I could write to you at length about all I have seen as it would interest you greatly. It is on a gigantic scale and no doubt about it. It is most interesting over here. I was out for a ride on my motorcycle this afternoon with Bob Murray. We stopped at a small inn for tea and I was able to get along OK with the girl who waited on us. She was quite pleased with my French.

Your loving son, Basil

France, Feb. 20/16

Dear Mother,

We are settled pretty well now in our new quarters. There are a fine bunch of officers here without a doubt and they are Canadians which is a whole lot.

A number of officers here are on their way up to the front. They are leaving tomorrow morning to go 'up the line' as they call it and they seem to consider it merely as a day's work. No one who has been in the trenches speaks of the tough side of it; they all take it so lightly. It seems funny that I am beating both Welland and Ramsey to it seeing that they joined up months before I did.

Those boots that father got me at Fraser's are the real thing. They are absolutely water-tight and are very comfortable.

Your loving son, Basil

Feb. 21/16

My dear Grace,

I am enjoying my stay here immensely as there are a splendid bunch of officers here, one of them reminds me very much of Ramsey. I suppose you are knitting hard at home now. If you could send me a pair of nice woollen gloves they would be very welcome indeed.

Write often because letters are very welcome. The next two months are the worst of the whole year in the trenches so I will need letters to keep my spirits up.

I am your loving brother,
Basil

P.S. I have a few minutes left, so I shall add a few lines. Let me know all about the little details of home – even little matters that may seem trivial to you – tell me about. It is now nearly two months since leaving home. I wonder how many more it will be till I am back again. B.

France – Feb.26/16

My dear Mother,

It is Saturday – nearly the beginning of a new week and I can hardly realize that a whole week has passed. We are now in billets behind the firing line.

I am sending you, if I ever get it off, a small necklace that I picked up. It is silver and I rather liked it. I hope you like it. There is a couple of inches of snow on the ground here today. We never move anywhere but we have terrible weather, and not to break the record we landed here with a heavy snow-storm driving in our faces.

The English officers we run across sometimes are very decent and sometimes are not. However for the most part I have been very much taken with them. This morning, asking the way from an M.P., he directed me as follows, 'Straight on to the Square, when you will see a statue of the Old Lady on the right' (meaning the Virgin). It struck me as ridiculous. There is a cross over my bed with three or four pictures on the wall in bright colours of different events in the Bible, so I won't become a heathen at any rate. This country is damnable – all flat for miles around and nothing to see but snow and wind mills. I have no idea when we will take our first turn in the trenches but it will be before very long.

Your loving son, Basil

1st Tunnelling Coy, C.E.F., 3rd Division, 2nd Army
Brit. Ex. Force, France
[Field Post Office 26 Feb./16]

Dear Father,

The above is our address here. It is the first time I have been able to send it to you. I am in a very nice house here. Roy Spencer and I are in this house and are very lucky. It is a small house; downstairs is the kitchen, sitting-room and dining room in one, and upstairs the bed-rooms. The owner of the house has a small butcher shop and grocery store adjoining. The men are in barns and very comfortable. Our section has a brick barn with a couple of feet of straw in it, good and warm and dry.

I don't know whether I told Mother about our adventures in getting here. At — we stopped for breakfast. There was no hot water for tea ready so we started to make it. The time passed quickly and before we knew what was happening the whistle blew and the train was off leaving half our company standing beside the track. We finished breakfast, marched to another station and got a passenger train – *some* looking outfit I can tell you, about 200 men, some in caps, others in sleeping caps, some with great-coats and puttees, some without, and a lot carrying tin boxes and dishes – the funniest sight imaginable tromping through the town to the station. We got a train, changed at another station and got to our destination.

Our officers' mess is in a place right behind our orderly room and the women that keep it are very cheery. Can you imagine just ten miles from the firing-line in a French village and in a French house having an officers' mess. Major Rogers was up to the front line this morning. We will go up for instruction soon into the trenches.

Father, I hope you do not worry over me. Everyone takes going into the trenches as a matter of course, so please just do the same.

Your loving son, Basil

France, Feb. 26/16

Dear Grace,

Well, ma sœur, I am getting to be a regular parlez-vous now. I get along OK with these people. I can talk more than I thought. A lot of the French I learned at school is coming back to me and I am learning some more. The people here address us as 'monsieur l'officier.' They are very decent to us and certainly can cook well. The coffee is excellent.

I surely think a lot about home and the good time I have had there. We have a mighty nice home I can tell you and Mother and Father have been mighty decent to us. I don't think we half appreciated what they did for us, do you?

I often try and figure out what you people will be doing at the same instant I am thinking. It is now 9:15 p.m. and 4:15 p.m. by your time. Pleasant dreams tonight and a goodnight kiss.

Your loving brother, Basil

Mar. 4th/16

My dear Mother,

As I write this letter on my bed I can hear the cannon constantly roaring up the line. I have got used to it, but when I am writing to you and so thinking of home, it has a very queer effect. I do not feel the least bit scared or anything like that, but just when I think that after each roar perhaps one or more men have passed into eternity, it is rather impressive.

Since my last letter I have had quite a few new experiences having been right up in the trenches. I will describe our trip from the time we left our base. We left one afternoon in motor lorries and came along a road through several towns to our base here. You can have no idea of the immensity of the whole thing until you actually see the army in working order. As we came along the guns gradually became louder until we could hear the distant explosions. We arrived in the afternoon and were allotted to our huts. As usual when we move it is raining, but our quarters are very comfortable. After dinner I went for a walk down the road. It was dark, of course, and very risky on account of the transports which have no lights and travel up the road at a good clip. They make a racket on the road so we know they are coming.

It was very weird to hear the roar of the cannon, the rumble of the wheels and about five or six hundred yards off the flares going up. The flares make a bright light and it is very pretty to watch them. Every little while we could hear a machine gun.

We went to bed about midnight but I could not get to sleep because shortly after I turned in, the guns started going fast and the whole place shook. The next morning we marched off and about half way to our advanced billets, we had to break up into small parties. We passed through a village which was pretty well in ruins. This place is shelled regularly and strange to relate, a number of civilians still live here.

In the afternoon the Germans began dropping shells over the field in front of our billets. It was rather interesting to hear the shriek of the shells and watch them explode. We are well sheltered and absolutely safe. Our first shift went to work almost right away. That night, Rankin, Spencer and I went up to the trenches about ten o'clock with a guide. It was a regular maze, but there is good walking as the communications trenches are in good shape with trench mats all the way. However if you step off, which I did regularly, you go into a foot or so of mud and water. The flares are life savers because they light up right to the back. The last ten minutes we walked over the open to our destination. I wish I could tell you about that but I dare not, we are not allowed to talk about our work even to officers outside the Tunnelling Company.

Needless to say, I was pretty muddy and wet when I got there as it was raining all the time. We came back about one a.m. over the open all the way as it is quite safe at night, the main danger being they often take a notion to drop a shell here and there or perhaps turn a machine gun on any part so you have to watch out. It was very exciting being so close to the Boches but it was terribly quiet in the dark night with the flares and once in a while a rifle shot or a machine gun. Every little piece you would suddenly hear 'halt' come out of the darkness. I surely halted, though I didn't see a sentry. The place is combed with trenches and when one sees all the barbed wire entanglements and everything, one wonders how on earth one side can ever get into the other's trenches at all. We saw a number of graves with plain wooden crosses, a mound of earth with these crosses, scattered all through the fields. I did not feel at all scared going into the trenches, just curious.

The dugout we have is very comfortable with a nice fireplace, and quite dry. No one is allowed to go out at night alone as we might get wounded by a stray shot.

Basil

Monavilla
1 Japan Road
Near Plank Avenue

Dear Mother,

Is that not a very swell address for my dwelling? It is some dwelling too, in fact one of the best dugouts along the line. It is dry, and although it has only a layer of two sandbags for cover on top, still I do not mind as nothing but rifle or machine-gun bullets hit it.

Roy Spencer and I have invested in some luxuries as you might call them and so we are very comfortable when up here; in fact, I would almost as soon be up here as at the billets.

Our dugout is about 12′ × 12′ and we can almost stand up in it. It has a wooden floor and is wood lined. On the front side we have a real door and a real window. In it there are two bunks, a table and several shelves. We have discarded the stove as it smoked too much, but we left the stove-pipe in for ventilation. We have bought an oil stove, an acetylene lamp, oil cloth for the table and have it all cleared out so we are very comfortable. Our work is very interesting for which I am glad as the ordinary trench routine of the infantry would be ghastly. I cannot tell you anything about our work.

Last night the battalion on this front sent out a patrol. The Germans had been putting some barbed wire entanglements out from their trenches with the probable intention of advancing their trenches. This patrol crawled over through no man's land, stole all the barbed wire and left a Belgian flag standing in its place. That was some stunt, don't you think? It is true because I saw the Belgian flag flying on the German wire myself. They lost one officer killed and one man wounded in doing it.

The shells were lighting pretty close to us this afternoon for a while, but no one was hit although we were splashed with mud a good deal and tonight going over to one of our shafts, when just getting off the dump [the material from the underground excavations], a machine gun started on it. We ducked mighty quick behind some cover.

Your loving son, Basil

Mar. 14/16

Dear Grace,

Please excuse this paper as it is all I have with me at present. The last couple of weeks I have been on the move so much that I have had no opportunities to write at all, scarcely. I was relieved in the trenches last night and am now back at the base resting. When I say the base it is a matter of a mile and a half from the trenches so we are by no means away from the noise which I would like to be for a while. I first went into the trenches up the line farther about two weeks ago. I took my turn in the trenches a couple of days after but it was cut short by an order for our section to move down the line further where our company was taking over from one of the original companies. It seems rather strange but we are not working on a Canadian front but on an Imperial and everyone seems surprised to see us down here. We have quite a bit of ground to cover and one point in particular is very interesting. As we are mining we can hear the Germans working there. When under ground that way it is a question as to who blows first.

Our dugout is very comfortable and thank goodness is dry. I take turns with Roy Spencer in staying out there. When one is out the other is at home resting. Things are a bit livelier than they were up the line and yesterday we had a bit of a bombardment. The Sgt. and I were going along the trench when two shrapnel burst just ahead of us. We were not touched but were splattered a bit with mud. You can tell pretty well where the shells are going and know when to duck, all except those blamed whizz bangs and they get a person's wind up a bit as they come so suddenly. The officers' dugout next to mine had one through the roof the other day but no one was inside luckily.

During the morning there is practically nothing doing – probably an occasional shell. About two or so in the afternoon one side or the other starts dropping shells into the other's trenches and of course there is retaliation. This generally keeps up to four-thirty or five. Then as dark begins to come on the machine guns start and they keep going most of the night with rifle fire as well. They play on the roads and any trucks they can see to try to catch carrying parties that go out at this time to bring up supplies. The working parties go out as well so the machine guns are pretty busy – they fire at everything that looks like a man. There is a machine gun which plays every night on the dump right near my dugout which makes an awful row when the bullets strike the ground.

I have only had three days' instruction in mining and I am rather over my depth here at present, seeing that we are up against some nasty problems. It does seem a bit out of place for me to be passing as a full-fledged mining officer when I never was down a shaft in my life until I hit the trenches.

I felt last night just as I felt once when I went home on leave from Kingston, but I had no one here to tell my troubles to and to cheer me up and I felt mighty homesick but fell asleep soon and feel OK this morning. Things were not going right and I had no one to help me out at all. However, Spencer arrived last night and I am going to go out tomorrow and stick around with him. I am finding out I know less than I thought I did.

This trench work is really not too bad. We have it on the infantry like anything as we can do something and so can keep interested. I have only been over here for a month and only in the trenches two weeks, but peace cannot be declared too soon. Up to the present I have not seen a man wounded or killed though there have been a few casualties around where we were – about one a day got by a sniper.

I received your box OK and it was in fine shape.

Your loving brother, Basil

France, March 16/16

Dear Mother,

It is just getting dark, a wonderful evening, just like spring at home, and it does seem so absurd that within a mile or two there is the firing line. I was looking out of the window for a while over some fields to the west of the town and could see puffs of black smoke where H.E. [high explosive] shrapnel was bursting. Everything should be peaceful here but instead the place is full of soldiers. I watched a bunch of youngsters playing. It does a chap good to get away from the khaki for a while. I could not help thinking of home tonight and I can tell you I would not mind being back there for a spell.

There were a lot of aeroplanes up today and they were shelled continually but none of them seemed to be hit. I saw an air fight but it did not amount to anything, both planes going home. I go back up to the trenches tomorrow afternoon.

I would almost as soon be up there as here, though we surely need a rest every so often.

With love, Basil

My dugout, France Mar 23/16

My dear Father,

You have been very good indeed in writing to me so often and I appreciate it very much. I get two of your letters to one of anybody else and they are very interesting letters. Please do not write anything about the war in them as I see enough of it but put in lots of news of home and the office. It is much nicer to hear about that. The town where my billets are is only a couple of miles back from the line. The place of course is pitch dark but there is one bright spot, a restaurant which is quite nice inside although it looks very bleak from the outside. There is an awfully decent bunch in these trenches now. We have scraped up an acquaintance with the trench mortar man who is from the West Indies.

I expect to go tomorrow for a rest to the billet as I have been out here for a week and one gets a bit tired of dodging bullets for a week steady. You should see the way I can flop down on my tummy when a machine gun plays in my direction. I have met men from every corner of the globe over here. These Imperial Tunnelling Companies are made up mostly of colonials, the officers I mean. The majority are from Canada or South Africa. The assistant controller of mines for this army corps was in

B.C. and knew Uncle Osborne fairly well. I have met several officers from B.C. who knew him. None of these English Canadians are going to stay in England after the war but are all going out to Canada again.

It is remarkable the feeling of confidence there is in all ranks over here. No one seems the least bit doubtful of the ultimate end, the only question is HOW LONG.

The Scotchmen have certainly lived up to their reputation in the fighting over here – no other corps, not even the crack English regiments dispute their title – wherever there is hard fighting you will always find the Gordons or the Black Watch.

It does seem strange for me to be 'mining officer' here when I never was down a shaft until I took charge over here on my shift. However, I have got onto the work pretty well now and don't imagine that there are Germans coming when I hear my heart beating.

Love to Grace and Mother
Your loving son, Basil

France, Mar. 25/16

My dear Father,

I have received all the parcels sent to me except the first one Grace sent. I am resting now, came in last night. I did not get up until eleven this morning and after lunch went down to the bath houses. These bath houses are great things. When the men come in from a spell in the trenches they get a bath and a complete change of underclothes, top shirt, towel and socks. The men certainly appreciate them. The baths are vats about 8′ × 10′ and two or three feet deep filled with warm water. Four or five men get in at a time. I think this is one reason for the good health of the troops. The men are all in good health and excellent spirits. I hope I get a shot at a German soon. So far I have not seen one.

I have a very good batman, a young chap about 20. I never have to tell him anything about my things. He stays with me all the time, goes up to the trenches with me and is always with me. He is an awfully nice kid.

Your loving son, Basil

(Letter addressed to Miss Grace Morris and stamped Field Post Office)
France, March 26th, 1916

Many thanks for the box and the hint. Here is a little souvenir, a piece of a German H.E. shell which blew our mess dugout to atoms and lit about 2′ from my bean when I was lying on my tummy trying to look like a keyhole or something still smaller.

B.M. Morris

France, Mar. 27/16

Dear Mother,

I have a beastly grouch on today. I do not know what is the matter. It is a dull wet day and cold. Yesterday was Sunday, but Sunday here is never different from any other day. I wish I could have a Sunday at home, go to church and have a nice read by the fireplace. You do now know how I long for that big room – it is one place I always think of – so comfortable and cosy.

We had our first casualties yesterday. Two men of our section were killed. A sausage lit on their dugout and killed them both. One was L. Corp. Mills from B.C. and the other Dan White from U.S. They were both young chaps, 18 and 21 years and were good men. We buried them last night after dark and I never will forget that scene. Behind the first line trenches about fifty yards in a slight hollow out of sight of the Germans. Their grave was dug and the Captain of the infantry company said a service over them, we five officers at one end, the firing party three on each side of the grave and the Captain at the other end. Flares going up all the time cast a light on the scene. There were no shots fired but the party presented arms and the graves were filled in.

Yesterday morning a meeting of officers was held and Major Rogers told us he had decided to resign. I like the Major very well personally and he has been very decent to me.

There was a terrible bombardment somewhere near here last night. It lasted for several hours and was one steady roar making all the houses shake and you could see only one wall of flame up the line. You have no idea what a feeling it gives a person not in it and I confess I felt very much like putting my head under the clothes like I used to do in a thunderstorm years ago.

I go back to the trenches tomorrow afternoon for another spell which I hope will not be as long as the last one.

Your loving son, Basil

France, Apr. 4/16

Dear Mother,

A Canadian mail came in yesterday and I was very lucky again. I intended to write last night but did not manage to do so and will have to cut this note very short as I am leaving for the trenches very shortly.

Lots of love, Basil

France, April 4/16

Dear Ramsey,

Just came out to the trenches for another spell today after a rest at the billet for a couple of days. It is really wonderful over here now, sunny and warm all the time, just like early June weather at home. It is rather hard to keep my mind on this letter just now as there is something doing up the line a piece. We can hear a steady roll of cannon and it has been going on since about four this afternoon. It is now nearly nine. Somebody is having a pretty hot time of it.

It was rather lively around our trenches here for a while this afternoon and a number got knocked out. I had a narrow shave when a shell hit about ten yards from me. It is a fact that you can hear it coming several seconds before it bursts and have time to take cover. I have had that same experience several times and have managed to get behind a transverse of a trench before it went off. Whizz-bangs of course you cannot get out of the way from. They are about the same size as our 18 PDRS [pounders] and are off before you can hear them coming. Rifle-grenades are rotten things too because you can neither hear them nor see them coming. The trench mortar stuff such as sausages, minnie-werfers and aerial torpedoes you can see coming but it is very hard to judge just where they will light.

We have been in now for over a month, we don't run all the risks that the infantry do as we never have to go over the parapet at night, but run the same risks from ordinary conditions. The shrapnel helmets they have now are great things. They have saved a lot of lives as the majority of shrapnel wounds are in the head. They are proof against the ordinary shell splinters or shrapnel bullets.

We have a good bunch of men with us, all good workers and willing. They are fine and we have some good N.C.O.'s.

Your loving brother, Basil

France, Apr. 6/16

Dear Mother,

I must apologize for the brief note I wrote a few days ago, but I was in a big hurry.

I am in the trenches now and will be here for a few days more. It is not bad to be in the trenches but too much at a stretch palls on a chap. You have to be careful all the time or else a sniper will get you. Some parts where you think you are in perfect safety and a bullet will whizz past your nut. Today I was reading some names on some graves, as I thought perfectly safe, and, ping, a bullet went past and hit the bank on the far side. I ducked, but had to laugh because if my number had been in that bullet I would never have heard it.

I have got quite used now to the sight of wounded men and some of them pretty badly at that. It made me feel a bit queer at first, but have got used to it now. This is not a cheerful line so I will not dwell on it.

The mice here are getting to be an awful nuisance and last night they ate up a number of our records. I am going to get a trap of some description as I am not going to waste ammunition on them.

McCammon had a mighty narrow escape the other day when a shell exploded in his dugout. I am sorry if I appear a bit blue in this letter, but, Mother, I know you will understand just how I feel. A person gets no sympathy in the army. I have had a nightmare the last two nights and woke up trembling all over. I had dreamed I was in a fight and was nearly bayonetted when I woke up. I don't know what caused such dreams. I hope I don't have one tonight.

I must close now as it is getting late and I have to be up bright and early as the controller of mines will be up to see us.

Your loving son, Basil

My dugout, 7/4/16

Dear Grace,

I came out this afternoon and have just finished supper. There is a show on somewhere around here as I can hear a steady roar of the guns and they have been going for some time. We had some stuff shoved over at us too today. I saw some of the wounded being taken out and it is rather rotten to see them. One chap had a slight wound in his leg and was quite cheerful as it meant a holiday for a while. A funny thing happened – we were out of the trenches on some open ground going over some work when we heard a shell coming. We all lay down flat just as it exploded about ten yards away – none of us were hit but as luck would have it, we flopped down in a mud puddle. McCammon had a mighty close shave. He was in his dugout when a shell hit right on it and exploded. Luckily, it hit an I-beam or he would have been no more. I was out on a run on my motorcycle yesterday afternoon. Over here is a good place to learn to ride. Everyone goes at a great clip. The country around is very pretty. What strikes me is the short distance between the towns which are only a couple of miles from the trenches. A lot of people stay in the towns; they do not mind the shells at all.

A machine gun plays right over our dugout every night. I thought there must be something wrong as I did not hear him at all tonight, but he has started just now.

Your loving brother, Basil

France, April 14/16

Dear Father,

I have been down at a school the past few days taking a course in rescue work for mines with the different apparatus used for working in gas and reviving men who have been overcome. We have had no use for it yet. It is very ticklish working under ground as quickly as possible and wondering where the Huns are. You hear sounds and try and locate them. Every noise in the gallery seems like a cannon going off there.

Basil

France, April 18/16

Dear Mother,

I am very sorry you were so long without letters. I wrote a lot from our base before we came up country, surely some of them got home.

Please, Mother, do not worry about me at all, as it will not do any good or keep me from getting hit. As the Tommies say, a shell won't get you unless your number is on it.

Lots of love, Basil

France, April 22/16

Dear Mother,

Have you ever lost your nerve? I nearly lost mine yesterday. I was up in the trenches when a straffe started. As I had been down for nearly two weeks without being in the trenches at all, it got my goat as the shells were coming close. My first impulse was to beat it down the communication trench, but I realized what I was doing and came back. I had to walk along the trench for a bit and after several had hit close to me, I was alright. Do you know it is a fact, though it may seem odd to you, that a person's nerves are better if he is right in a thing like that and has a couple of close shaves. There is nothing harder to do than to sit in a trench when they are shelling and do nothing. You begin to think, will the next one get me?

Our new O.C. Captain North, a Canadian, is here now and taking over the Company. He seems to be a very capable man and very decent as well.

Tomorrow is Easter Sunday and it will be a pretty queer Easter for me. However, we will make the best of it. Let me know when Ramsey comes over so I can write to him in England.

This will be all for now, Basil

France, April 24/16

Dear Mother,

This being Easter Monday, it is a holiday for the French people living here and they are sporting around in their best togs.

The roads are dusty now although we had a steady rain for a week. It surely made the trenches in an awful condition and there is lots of water in them.

Don't worry over me as I am feeling fine and am alright.

Your loving son, Basil

France, April 27/16

Dear Mother,

We are leaving here before long, moving to another part of the line. That does not mean very much to you.

We have had quite a bit of excitement here lately and I wish I could tell you all about it but that is not possible.

Our casualties are mounting up and are more than twenty now. Sgt. McDonald has gone nutty over it and it is fierce to watch a big husky man like that jump whenever a door slams. He used to be so cheerful and now he looks scared all the time. He likely will be sent to the base for shell shock.

Stuart Thorne is in charge of No. 1 Section. I am very glad to see it as he is an awfully good man and very decent. I think that he is one of the best men we have in our Company. On the whole we have a very good bunch of men and officers and we are pulling well now. I am in the office and will be back on the line again soon. I have to stay here to do the draughting at this end of the work until we get a draughtsman.

Do you know whenever I think of home the picture that presents itself is the sitting-room with a fire in the grate, Father sitting at the centre table with his spectacles on reading a paper and glancing up every once in a while to say 'Listen' and proceeding to read some piece that has caught his fancy, Grace at the piano playing and you by the fire knitting. How I long to be back there for one evening at least. You do not know how a chap, when he comes down from the trenches, longs for a few hours at home.

Lots of love to everyone, Basil

France, April 28/16

Dear Grace,

You and Mother have been calling me down for not writing enough to you at home. If I write any oftener, I will have to get a private secretary.

It is fine weather now and everything is nice and green and very pretty along some of these roads, with a level stretch of white road ahead and tall trees bordering it along each side. This should be a nice country in peace time, I think, as everything is so picturesque.

I had quite a ride on my motorcycle this afternoon. I had a breakdown about halfway home and dropped into one company headquarters to get fixed up. The damn fool broke the gas control and I couldn't throttle the blamed thing down under about thirty miles an hour. It was some fun getting the rest of the way.

The Huns sent over a bunch of Lydite [lyddite] shells the other night and it is fierce stuff. The stuff is not poisonous but makes your eyes smart and run water. It will blind you for a couple of hours if you get much of it.

I am in the best of health and spirits and never felt better. Don't worry over me at all. I am happy.

My love to everyone, Basil

France, April 28/16

Dear Father,

It is wonderful over here now. Spring is here in earnest and everything is lovely and green. It is just as hot here now as it is in June at home.

Major Rogers has left us and has gone to the C.R.R. [Canadian Railroad] Construction Company and our new C.O. is Capt. North.

Thorne has now got charge of No. 1 Section and I am glad to see it as I think he will be a good officer to have charge of a section. You have no conception of what a trench looks like after a heavy bombardment. It is all craters and mounds with no marks of a trench practically left and is fierce. Imagine what a hundred guns or more trained on about a hundred yards of trench would do in a couple of hours steady firing. This very seldom happens of course.

I am going to turn in, your loving son, Basil

France, May 6/16

Dear Mother,

I got your Easter parcel and the church one yesterday so you see I was quite lucky. They were both fine and came in mighty handy. In the church one I got a khaki shirt, a khaki handkerchief, fifty cigarettes, two pairs of socks and a bunch of chocolate and gum so I think I fared very well. That stuff you sent me came in handy too as I was just out of some of it. It takes parcels a week or two longer to get here than letters. We have our mess fixed up fine now and everything is quite comfortable.

We have a gramophone which is very good too. I wish I could go to a dance tonight. It seems ages since my last dance, the one in the Town Hall.

All our officers now have permanent passes which are good anywhere in the British area. Being in the Tunnelling Company surely has its advantages. We have motorcycles and permanent passes and our work is much more interesting than the infantry.

The most disliked officer anywhere in the trenches is the trench mortar officer. It gives a good description of him in 'The First Hundred Thousand' [by Ian Hay]. In fact, that book surely is true to life and describes everything mighty well. These cartoons by Bairnsfather also are very good and true to life.

Leave for us should start in another three weeks and will be welcome as one most certainly gets fed up on the trench life. It is very fascinating to think of when back in Canada, but the fascination mostly all goes after we are here a couple of months. We are all in the best of health and spirits.

Lots of love, Basil.

France, May 9/16

Dear Grace,

I got a couple more letters in the mail yesterday, one from you, one from mother and an Easter egg from Mrs. May. She sent each of us an egg (I got the two Easter parcels OK).

My batman, McGuire, a youngster of 18, had some very bad news yesterday. His father had died. It is pretty tough on the chap and he is pretty blue.

We have had numerous changes in our company lately. Billy May is adjutant again, Thorne is O.C. #1 Sect., McMillan O.C. #2, Bob Murray no longer being in charge of it, Spencer O.C. #3, Morley being no longer in charge of it, and Ron King still has #4. The O.C. used good judgement I think in selecting the new section commanders.

Must close now, Basil

May 11/16

My dear Mother,

I have not written to you for quite a while as I have not had much opportunity to write. I got five big bundles of socks today and they surely made quite a display. I will give them out to the men soon. Thanks very much for them, at least thank Grace for me.

One of our sgts. has got the D.C.M. [Distinguished Conduct Medal] and two privates military medals. They got them today. They surely deserved to get them. After a heavy bombardment the other day, our saphead was broken in and a bunch of our men and one officer buried in the galleries. The galleries began to fill with water and these three men swam or rather had to crawl for thirty feet underwater to get to the pumps and work them until they were dug out which was about eighteen hours afterwards. They did not know how far underwater they would have to go when they started or whether the hose would be broken when they got there or what was up. We are the first Canadian Tunnelling Company to get any decorations. This tunnelling game is mighty interesting and mighty creepy as well. It is away ahead of the infantry I think. Next to the trench mortar officer, I think comes the mining officer in unpopularity as the infantry do not like miners a little bit.

These peasants over here have some splendid big horses. I have never seen such fine horses before and they all look well cared for. You never see a skinny or dejected looking horse.

Jeffery has gone to hospital with lumbago. At this rate, we won't have many of the old crew left soon. We are getting some new officers in here soon on probation. I have managed to hang on to the Company so far. I hope I can stick with the Company as it would be rotten to be fired, but being young (most of the mining officers here are over 28) and inexperienced, there is a chance. I hope I make good, however, but have no chance for promotion of any sort (whatever). The work is mighty interesting however and I like it.

Our leave has started now. It will be quite a while I am afraid till mine will be due. What I would not give if I could get home.

Lots of love, Basil

5 ❅ The home front ❅ ❅ ❅ ❅ ❅ ❅ ❅

In August 1914, when war broke out, my father had decided that Ramsey, as the eldest son, should be the first to go overseas to defend his country. But it didn't work out that way.

From the time he and his friends had learned that Canada was at war, Ramsey's only ambition had been to take part in this great adventure. Having received his commission in the 42nd Lanark and Renfrew militia regiment, he had joined the 38th Battalion, known by the men in it as the 'Royal Ottawas,' and had been sent for training to Barriefield camp near Kingston.

But in the following summer, 1915, instead of being sent overseas, the battalion was sent to Bermuda to relieve an Imperial regiment for service in France. For the soldiers of the 38th, Bermuda was an unexpected interlude, an earthly paradise far from the guns of Flanders. Ramsey sent home for his Peterborough canoe, which he used to advantage in his social life. The months passed by swiftly and peacefully.

Ramsey's company was stationed at St David's; in a letter to Basil, then still at Barriefield, he described his life there.

19 Aug. [1915]

Dear Basil,

Am acting adjutant this week. Heard you lost a company – hard luck. But it can't be helped. Stick to the regiment as long as you can – going with a draft you don't know where you are going to go and it pays to stick with your O.C. as long as you can. We were due for a draft but by coming to Bermuda we came intact and in toto.

St. David's is a desert island, the extreme end of the Bermudas. The nearest town, St. Georges, is a mile away and Hamilton, the capital, 12 to 15 miles by road. You take a ferry to St. Georges. Fishing off the coral reefs occupies most of the time of the people, white and coloured. We swim on a good sandy beach and are independent, in fact we are Gov's of the island. Bermuda is O.K., but a good part of the time smells like a drug store after sundown when the mists begin to rise. Active mosquitos and noisy crickets but we sleep under mosquito nets. We like it. Am sending a few pictures. Write and tell me all about Barriefield Camp.

Ramsey

Ramsey remained in Bermuda all winter. In January he suggested that my mother and I might come for a holiday at a hotel near where he was stationed.

Dear Grace – 30 January, 1916

The St. George's Hotel is quite a good one and military people get rates at all hotels. Do you know that a naval or military officer can get a dinner or any meal or a bedroom at the Hamilton (Bermuda's classiest hotel) for a dollar. We are really awfully popular around the big hotels, particularly on Tuesday and Saturday at the Hamilton or Thursday at the Princess when they have their big balls. They like to have us stick around. Uniforms cut a very big figure at those affairs I can tell you. Every Wednesday there is a dance at the St. George's. You would both like it awfully well. You'll forget there ever was a war. People here are all of the very butterfly type, and with so many Americans you'll forget all about it. You'll go back to Canada, where all the most excellent people come from, absolutely content to never leave it again. It will really do you a lot of good. I never liked Canada like I do now. The quality of the people, their sanity, charm of manner, vigour and everything compares very favourably with these enervated fool Bermudians and loud squacking Americans. You will know it later.

Bermuda is really wonderful now, you will like it awfully well and come before the end of February. Bermudian girls dress rummily so don't worry. Lots of clothes for tennis or roughing it and a ball dress or two. You will be O.K. I know.

Your loving brother,
Ramsey

We did not go to Bermuda. Although we gave it serious consideration, in the end we decided that there was too much war work to be done at home to take a holiday at this time. In April, after Basil had been in France for a couple of months, Ramsey wrote the following letter.

Dear Grace – St. Georges, Bermuda – 30 April
    You will no doubt be tickled to get one more rummy letter to add to your collection, but I will really write a lot more fluently and more frequently a little later on getting to England or en route. We are likely to go at a fairly early date now.
    I am enclosing all Basil's letters. Basil writes very well indeed. He didn't describe it quite so luridly to me, and to tell you the truth it made me feel a little sick around the stomach at first, but now I am getting used to the idea of having B. poking around in the middle of it all. He is all to the good I can tell you. I like getting letters from B. with such a healthy outlook on it all. He will probably win promotion and all kinds of rewards and will undoubtedly earn it all.
    We are likely to get over pretty quickly now. That makes me feel a lot better. We are getting very little leave now because we will probably go 3 or 4 weeks before my next birthday, probably before June.
                                                    Y.L.B. Ramsey

Meanwhile, at home in Pembroke, everybody seemed to be involved in war work because of the proximity of the military camp at Petawawa, where the Canadian artillery was being trained. As the artillery was a most important branch of the army in the Great War, this meant thousands of men practically on our doorstep.
    The large canteen required many volunteers every day of the week, from early morning until late at night. Older women from the Red Cross were in charge, with many younger women assisting them. Every morning a party of twenty or more drove out to the camp and spent the day in the booths selling soldier comforts. My duty, one day a week, consisted of dishing out vast quantities of apple pie and ice cream. It was a welcome sound when the bugle played the 'Last Post' and lights went out in all the tents throughout the camp.
    The large Red Cross rooms were busy every day with women knitting socks, Balaclava caps, fingerless gloves, and long scarves, and rolling bandages and sewing pyjamas. Under the supervision of my mother and

Mrs Williams, the mother of our friend Welland, large wooden boxes were packed with supplies for hospitals and sent overseas. One group of women working for the Red Cross, including my mother, called itself the Pembroke Needle Battalion; a picture of this group appeared in a Montreal paper and in some way reached the trenches, to the great amusement of Basil and the other officers who had been at Pembroke. Most fundraising events, such as raising money for the Red Cross work, were undertaken by the men of the town, assisted by the women in various ways.

A local chapter of the Imperial Order Daughters of the Empire was organized by Mrs E.A. Dunlop. Many active young women belonged, and assisted in Red Cross work as well as providing concerts for the men at the camp. At the concerts we sang, danced, and occasionally produced a colourful chorus line; one of the most successful songs was 'Won't You Wait Till the Cows Come Home' from a current New York show.

As the gunners swarmed into town, especially at the weekend, they made great use of the soldiers' club held in the auditorium of the town hall. Here women cooked 'home-made' snacks and great quantities of bacon and eggs. It was a place to relax, get a good meal, and write letters home. At the same time, soldiers of all ranks were entertained at various houses throughout the town, especially in those homes whose sons were serving in the overseas army. In many homes, there was 'open house' on Saturday evenings for young soldiers, gunners, and officers, some of whom came with letters of introduction from distant friends. The matter of rank was handled by the men themselves. For example, a group from one battery, consisting of the commanding officer and several NCOs, came to our house all one summer; they planned their visits for alternate weekends, so there would be no embarrassment to the hostess. British Army rules were still in effect.

The war completely changed the social life of the town. In the summer, as usual, people went to their cottages, and there were still tennis parties on Saturday afternoons, but the players were mostly young women. There were few young men not in uniform and for most of these there seemed to be an excuse, a physical handicap or the necessity to complete an education, especially if one was studying to become a doctor.

In July 1916 I went to visit Mary Rogers at the Coniagas Mine in Cobalt. It was an experience to remember. Mary had come to this mining camp when she was a bride of seventeen, one of the first white women to live in Cobalt. She now had three pretty children with a nursemaid to look after them while she took part in all the activities of the town. She did everything with great vehemence, gardening, playing tennis, riding her horse, and working at the Red Cross rooms. Her company was always stimulating.

On this, my first visit to a mining town, I found a number of things that surprised me. The roadways wandered over the rocks and the plank sidewalks wound their way past structures called shaft houses. One such sidewalk arrived at a flight of steps leading to the verandah of the mine manager's house of the Coniagas Mine; surprisingly, beyond the house was a beautiful stretch of green lawn bordered by beds of flowers.

Not far away, over barren rocks, lay the Trethewey Mine, which had been managed by Stuart Thorne before he went to war. As I looked at the forbidding landscape I wished that I had known him then, and his sister Elsie who was spoken of with great affection (she went to England as a V.A.D. and worked with blind soldiers at St Dunstan's in London during the war).

Almost immediately I was engulfed by warm hospitality, and treated as an honoured guest. The Coniagas Mine manager took me underground wrapped in a slicker and rainproof hat, down by elevator to a very deep level. Now the terms used by Basil in his letters from France had much more meaning; apparently in hunting for silver or for Germans underground, the mining techniques were much the same.

On the surface there was a lively social life. It was not that people forgot about the men who were facing death every minute of every day in the trenches, but to sustain those men life had to be lived in as normal a fashion as possible. The annual tennis tournament of the north country was now taking place in Haileybury, Cobalt's sister town. Tennis was the popular game of the moment and most social life centred around it. Many of the mines had excellent clay courts and in fine weather the day's entertainment would be tennis with luncheon.

I entered the tournament and with good luck reached the finals in ladies' singles, but here my success came to an end. The match was won by a most attractive American woman, the wife of the manager of the great Nipissing Mine. She dressed with impeccable taste in clothes from New York and entertained graciously. Everyone was delighted that the silver cup was to remain in Cobalt but with no hard feelings towards me, the outsider who had tried to take it away. The winner gave a most elegant luncheon in my honour. Some of the women I met there became my friends and remained so for many years.

While much was being done for the soldiers in training in Canada, those at the fighting front and in the ships at sea were always foremost in people's thoughts. A steady stream of letters and parcels was the answer, and it was remarkable that they could be delivered to the soldiers so far away in the trenches. Parcels of hand-knitted socks and tins of fudge were greeted with enthusiasm, but nothing equalled letters with news of home. And to the people at home, letters from the front were most precious. The scrawls in pencil on flimsy paper, sometimes marked 'opened by censor,' were treasures to be guarded with care.

This letter came from a cousin:

Flanders, 3/1/16

Dear Grace,

Everything was at a standstill along the line around Christmas, hardly a gun fired for days. To the south of us the French seemed to keep up the usual racket. There was nothing like the unofficial truce of Christmas, 1914, although the Germans attempted to get friendly with a few of our battalions. They came out of their trenches and walked over to the barbed wire motioning for our fellows to come out and play. They were told to get back as there was nothing doing in the line of friendship. It took a few rounds from a machine gun to make them return to their lines. After that they stuck up white flags along the top of the trench and sat on the parapet. This seemed to amuse them, so our men left them alone for the day. It just happened that the battalions that the Germans tried to get friendly with were two which suffered heavily in the gas attack at Ypres.

This country is simply a big swamp, mud and water everywhere. The men in the trenches are wonderful the way they stick it. Marching back to billets after four days in the front line the men are plastered with mud from head to foot.

Your cousin, Bill Ross

Bill Ross was with the Post Office, getting letters and parcels to the trenches. He survived the war.

March 28/16

Dear Grace,

Please excuse the frightful paper and pencil, but I can't get anything better in this hole. I received your welcome letter the other day and the candy two days later, also very welcome as you may suppose. It was in perfect condition ... Thank you very much indeed for your thoughtfulness.

Well, in spite of my eminently peaceful proclivities, I find myself somewhere in France at an advanced dressing station. I enjoy it very moderately, though there is no doubt the work is better near the line. We have a very comfortable billet whose only disadvantage lies in the proximity to shell fire. The first question to be answered about a shell I find is whether it is your own or a Boche. This takes time and experience. Our other great annoyances are the anti-aircraft guns which treat our roof to a peppering when going at our aeroplanes. However, I just had to take a couple of toddles up into the trenches to realize we have no cause to grumble and are very lucky.

Yours, Ambrose

Ambrose Moffat was my teenage friend. He was in the Army Medical Corps and survived the war.

Belgium, May 22/16

Dear Grace,

I am in the line again. This is my third trip in and Fritz hasn't got me yet but you never can tell. He has hit me though. It was last night and I must tell you how it happened. I was standing talking to one of our corporals when suddenly, I felt something hit me on the leg like a small stone. I crawled around to see if I could find what hit me and suddenly felt something hot – found it was a German bullet, a spent bullet. If it had hit me before it struck the ground, I would probably have had a 'Blighty' but no such luck!

Your cousin, Welland

Welland Williams, my riding friend in Pembroke, was killed at Vimy Ridge in April 1917.

Trenches, 28/7/16

Dear Grace,

Received your letter of July 3rd the night before last and was very
pleased to know that you had not forgotten me. The socks were just fine
and came at the right time as I had just about worn out the lot I brought
over with me. Regarding the 'Mutt and Jeffs,' you know how I used to
enjoy them, and to have them come over the sea was a surprise and joy
combined, and for days after I received them, I carried them around in
my pocket and used to show them to all the officers I met and I can tell
you we all had a good many laughs over them. I showed them to several
English officers but they could not see the jokes, but a Canadian gets a
barrel of fun out of them. They were thoroughly enjoyed by a good
many soldiers in Flanders.

I started this letter in the trenches but was interrupted. My four days
rest did not pan out as such as I had a lot of work to do at headquarters.
Go back tomorrow night for four days in the trenches. It's a great life.
About 2:30 in the afternoon I go up and never have anything but my
coat and neck-tie off for the time I am in. Plan on twelve hours sleep in
four days. Between climbing up and down the wet holes in the ground
and stumbling in shell holes in the dark, occasionally dodging shells,
machine-gun or rifle fire, we have an interesting time and are generally
glad to get back to headquarters.

Basil is on the shift opposite me and I only see him when we are
changing. He was on duty up there when the Huns blew a mine and the
O.C. speaks very highly of the way he acted. We were mentioned in dispatches for the general attitude of the company and Basil was the leading
light.

It's wonderful in a good many ways. You see sights that you would
deem impossible. Take Ypres for example, a town much bigger than
Ottawa and all the buildings of brick and stone, and I don't think there is
one building left in the place. I have seen several places wiped off the
map. All there is left is the macadam roads. This will be a great country
for a construction engineer after the war.

Bob Murray

Bob Murray, a mining engineer from the Maritimes, whom I met when
the Tunnellers were in Pembroke, was awarded the Military Cross and
survived the war.

All these letters were dear to me, but none more so than Basil's.

France, May 12/16

My dear, darling, devoted, dovey, dainty, delightful, not to mention dutiful sister,

How can I begin to thank you enough for the socks you sent me? They started to come yesterday. Can you imagine me wandering from the orderly room over here with five big bundles in my arms and again today with four? I will be dreaming socks for the next week or two ... They are mighty nice socks and will come in very handy indeed. Each man will get two pairs. They will be mighty thankful for them as in the saps they get wet continually.

My fears about getting fired are no longer justified. I am going out on the line again in a few days with No. 3 section under Spencer. I am glad to get in it as I like working under Spencer.

A very funny thing happened the other day on McMillan's work. He was going up the trenches with a company commander (infantry) and the Padre (chaplain) ahead of him when the Huns started sending over some sausages. Mac stopped but they kept on going until some dropped fairly close and they ducked into a dugout. When it slackened Mac discovered they had ducked into our magazine and here was the Padre sitting on a box of gun cotton and the company commander on a box of powder. When he told them they made one dive for the door and up the trench.

We wear these steel helmets now. I suppose you have seen pictures of them, ungainly looking but mighty useful.

Your loving brother, Basil

France, May 18/16

Dear Mother,

I got your parcel OK and thanks very much for it. I especially like the maple sugar and wish I could have some of it on toast like we used to have on the verandah.

I am 21 tomorrow and it seems strange when I look around the mess at the other officers. I feel such a kid. McMillan and Rankin are over 40 and all the rest are over 26. It is rather funny that I should be here. The O.C.'s favourite name for me is 'Youngster.' Spencer, my O.C. of No. 3 section is a mighty fine chap. I wish you knew him.

I am in charge of building the new huts. I run up every morning on my motorcycle and back at night, close to sixty miles a day, so I am pretty tired at night as these pave roads are pretty rough.

Lots of love, Basil.

Belgium, June 12/16

Dear Grace,

I wrote a few days ago a very brief letter so I am writing again today. I go on leave to Blighty tomorrow morning. I wish either you or Ramsey would be in England while I am there.

Everything is going fine here now. You should see our mess room now – quite a fine place with a fireplace and lots of comfortable chairs etc. Our O.C. is responsible for it. He surely is a prince.

You should see our steel helmets when up in the trenches. They surely are very funny looking just like inverted soup bowls. Simpson had a shell burst nine feet from him (a whizz bang) and a big piece hit his helmet. He was knocked down but not hurt at all.

Love, Basil

Basil got his leave as planned and crossed the Channel on June 13. In the meantime, Ramsey's battalion, the 38th, had completed its task of defending Bermuda and finally crossed the Atlantic. They were now in camp in England and, with great good luck, Ramsey was also due for leave. Thus the two brothers were able to spend several days together in London, where they had 'a glorious time' and not 'a minute to spare.'

6 ❈ All in the game ❈ ❈ ❈ ❈ ❈ ❈ ❈

Basil returned to the front in late June 1916; it would be four months before his next leave – months of intense fighting in the Ypres salient. The Tunnellers were proving their worth. On July 24 Major North was able to give warning that an enemy mine was about to be blown up under the Allied trenches: the next morning a terrific discharge removed a huge section of the forward defences, but because of the warning the casualties were light and the enemy attack failed; the crater, 450 feet long by 160 feet wide, was seized by the Canadian infantry.

In mid-August Basil noted that he had been at the front for six months, which made him a 'veteran.' His old life in Canada seemed a faraway dream, the war itself the only reality. Increasingly his letters expressed homesickness and loneliness; tired and bored with the war, 'fed up on the whole business,' he was dreading another winter in the trenches.

Ramsey finally made it to France in August and had the good fortune to be based at first near Basil; thus the brothers were able to see each other from time to time. On September 21, while Basil and his friend Bob Murray were strolling behind the lines off duty, they ran into Ramsey by accident. In Bailleul for tea, they had their picture taken together and sent it home: the bright, happy youths we had known now looked like the trench-weary soldiers they had become. Although cheered by Ramsey's presence, Basil also worried about him, for he knew the dangers faced by the infantry.

June 27/16

Dear Father,

My letters to you are very scarce and far between but I am sure you will understand. I came down from the trenches last night and it was an

awful night too – dark as pitch, raining and plenty of mud. I left the dugout having been relieved by Brown about midnight and walked down to
the road which is about two miles back from the line. I only fell into one
shell hole on the way down and it was full of water. The lorrie was waiting there for us and we got back to camp about 2 a.m. I had a wonderful
sleep and did not get up until noon, and even then felt as if I could sleep
all day long. In the trenches we have to sleep with all our clothes on
except our boots and with our revolvers and gas helmets right at our side
as there is no telling what is going to happen.

Our front is very unsettled and matters are especially uneasy for us
that way. We have to work very hard too, getting to bed generally
between two and three in the morning and up again by seven-thirty, so
when you have four or five days of this at a stretch a chap is pretty well
all in when he comes down for a rest.

I was out in no man's land the other night with Captain Spencer for a
while and it is a very nice feeling to be out there. I did not go across to
the German trenches but was just out a piece from our own parapet. It is
not as hard to be in a field when they are shelling as to be in a trench.
Because in the latter case, you are cramped and have to sit and do
nothing. You have no idea how hard it is to take a shelling. We were
through a small straffe yesterday afternoon. It is quite a sight to watch
the trench mortars going and coming. You can watch them all the way.
The Hun's minniewerfers or minnies as they are called look like a stick
of wood coming over turning end for end.

I hope that everything is coming along all right and that the office is
going well. I am glad that Grace is going on a holiday this summer as she
needs it. She has worked hard and steadily. I think you and Mother
should take one too somewhere. Hope you will write as often in the
future as you have done in the past.

> Your loving son, Basil M. Morris

> France, June 27/16

Dear Mother,

I was glad to get your interesting letter today. I was not in the big
show here, thank goodness, but had a grandstand seat for it and saw it
all. It was a wonderful sight. Just like a Toronto Exhibition fireworks display. As you say, there was one company – hardly any of their men who
were in the trenches got out. We relieved them about three weeks before

on the front where we are now working. Where we are is pretty warm at times and we have lost a number of men but hope that we will be lucky in the future.

It was great being on leave in London with Ramsey and we had a very good time.

I have run across pretty nearly everyone I ever knew over here, Joe McCool and Fred Kenning [from Pembroke], and yesterday in the trenches I saw Duke West and a couple of other chaps I knew at varsity.

I thought I was going down for the count yesterday but escaped. They were shelling a road I was going along with H.E. shrapnel. However, I got to the ditch before one exploded not ten yards from me and I heard the stuff whistle over my head. It is mighty lucky that one can hear those shells coming as we have a slight chance then.

I am down for four days rest now after five days in the trenches.

Lots of love, Basil

July 3/16

My dear Mother,

I wrote the other day but thought I would write again. It is raining and very bleak – the guns are booming up on the line and everything is disconsolate. The only thing that is very cheering is the news from down south [the beginning of the first Battle of the Somme] and it surely is cheering. However, I cannot help feeling blue and rather homesick. You do not know how much I would like to be back home tonight.

Everyone over here is talking about being home for Christmas but that is not possible at all as there is lots of hard work here yet for all of us and I only hope that I will be lucky enough to pull through this affair with a whole skin. We all have been very lucky so far and I hope will be just as lucky in the future.

McCammon, who was back in England for three months with shell shock is over here with us again. You would not know this company now it has changed so much. Thorne is sick in hospital in London and we don't know when he will be back. We have a lot of new officers. Major North is our new O.C. and Jim Rattray is our adjutant. I am no longer junior officer in the company which is quite a satisfaction, but am nearly halfway up the list. Won't it be great when this row is all over? It will likely be quite a while yet. However, we in the trenches do not know any more about the general outlook than you people do.

I wish you could see some of the things over here. They are beyond imagination.

Lots of love, Basil

France, July 3/16

Dear Grace,

I am enclosing a few snapshots which were taken when in London. Jack [Hope] and I were down to dinner at Dr. Stewart's house in Surbiton.

I just came down from my turn in the trenches last night. There has been a lot doing around here for the past week or so and it has been very interesting. Things are going well and everything is rosey with us. McCammon came back last night again and he was glad to get back to us.

Most of the 59th are over here now and nearly all are in the Brigade which is working on our front. I am continually running across chaps in the trenches who speak to me.

Love, Basil

July 11/16

Dear Grace,

I am very blue and ill at ease tonight and feel very, very lonely. I wish I were at home tonight and could talk to you and get you to play. I came down from the trenches during the night and got back here about 3:30 a.m. as it was breaking day. I was glad to get down as I had been working hard and was quite tired.

I got your parcel today and was very glad to get the salted almonds. They really are great.

Love, Basil

July 12/16

Dear Grace,

I wrote to you the other night but it was a very short letter. Received the parcel with the shirt in it. The shirt is fine really but how did you expect me to put a collar on it as you had a button on the neck instead of button holes. It is easily seen that you are not in the shirtmaking trade. We have a cute little kitten here now, a nice grey one. It is the only survivor of a large and prosperous family who were all killed by shell fire and we had this one brought down to camp.

I have been down now for two days. I do not mind going up very much even if I nearly got croaked a couple of times. It is all in the game. You are very good writing so often. Letters really are the only things we have to look forward to over here. A chap gets used to it however and does not mind it very much. Just the same, I get pretty nervous sometimes. Write often.

Your loving brother, Basil

July 15/16

Dear Mother,

I am going back up the line tomorrow evening. I had a couple of letters today from Canada which made things more cheerful looking. I have not left camp lately. I know the country around here pretty well now. It is all more or less the same wherever you go. Give me Canada every time instead of this place. If I ever go travelling after the war, I certainly shall leave this part of northern France severely alone.

Will you send me sometime any new snaps Grace has taken as I like to get them. The snaps she sent of Father are some of the best I ever saw of him.

I would like to be home for some of the dances this summer and some of the picnics. I get so homesick sometimes thinking of them I could almost croak. It is alright when up in the trenches as we are so busy there but down here we have nothing to do so I get rather lonesome.

Love, Basil

July 19/16

Dear Mother,

I came down from the trenches last night and had a great old sleep this morning. I did not get up until noon and surely enjoyed my sleep. We had quite a job last night to get through here as Heinie started to throw around a bunch of stuff in our direction just as we were coming down.

We lost a number of men the last time up, nothing to speak of in a way, as they were all wounded, but still it was rather hard luck. Two of them are very serious but the others not too bad. They were a game crowd, and one young chap only 18 or so, whose knee was completely shattered and his arm nearly off, never even groaned while we were fixing him up and taking him away. The only thing was he said it was a shame to leave him lop-sided, and asked Simpson to write to his mother. I don't think he has much chance of getting better however.

Some time ago I mentioned that Sgt. Johnson, who won the D.C.M., was very seriously wounded. No one expected him to pull through, but since then we have heard that he is pulling through alright. It is funny how some men can pull through when it looks hopeless for them. I hope if I get mine at any time I will have grit enough to stand it the way those chaps did. It gave me a tight feeling in my throat to see those chaps smashed up and a small chance of recovery and yet never complaining and hardly a groan when they must have been suffering something fierce as the perspiration was pouring off them.

I saw Archie and Sam McDougall the last time I was down here resting and may look them up again if I have a chance to go around their way. Everything is rosy – Hope you all are quite well and don't work too hard.

Love, Basil

July 20/16

My dear Grace,

We have been down now for three days. I really am getting terribly fed up on the whole business and wish it was all finished as it gets so very tiresome. You cannot realize what it is like back home, but only have a hazy idea of it. Do you remember John Leslie Thomson at Kingston last summer? He was killed last night. A bullet hit him in the bean, or rather two did. Two bullets from two different directions got him at the same time. I guess he never knew what hit him.

After six months out here a person can call himself a veteran and in about three more weeks we will be out here that long. I feel now as if I had been out here fighting the Huns all my life and that Canada and all the old life is only a dream. However, it must end sometime and we will be back there again and all this over here will be only a memory and probably time will smooth out my sad recollections and leave only the bright spots.

I long for that home of ours a whole lot at times. I never appreciated my home when I was there until I left the place. However, we are out here to beat the Hun and not to worry about things that cannot be.

When you run across chaps who have given up everything to come out here it makes a chap think a whole lot. I did not make much of a sacrifice and am young, but there are lots of men up in years who have thrown up everything to come to this place and they surely deserve all the credit that is coming to them.

Stuart Thorne came back a couple of weeks ago. He was sick for a while in England but is alright again. You might send me, please, a tin of Hudson's Bay tobacco, some cigarettes, shaving powder and some late copies of the Saturday Evening Post, which has some awfully good stories.

Lots of love, Basil

July 27/16

Dear Mother,

I just came down from the trenches last night. I am having an extra day down this time which naturally I am glad of. This four days up and four days down makes me rather tired sometimes and I want to get clear away from it all for a while. I would like to get right back in the bush somewhere in Canada where I would never see a uniform and no talk about the war at all. I may be writing some rather blue letters to you lately but do not take them seriously. I get homesick and lonesome down in camp. I miss home very much. It certainly clears up the atmosphere a whole lot to tell someone my troubles and get a bit of sympathy.

Things go on here day after day just the same old way and there is really nothing now to write to you about very much. We have a lot of new officers and they are a very decent crowd. A chap, Charlie Morris, from Toronto is here – a very decent chap. I went through varsity with his brother. We have very interesting work and I am mighty glad that I didn't come over with the infantry.

July 28/16

It is really a gorgeous day today, sunny and warm. These days are rather scarce over here. I had a big mail from Canada yesterday, about eight letters all told. I go down for a bath this afternoon. We have fine baths over here, nice shower baths with warm water. The only thing is I would like to get in for a swim in a river or something.

Love, Basil.

July 29/16

Dear Grace,

According to the latest official reports you have departed for a while to Cobalt. Be sure and don't fall down a shaft up there. It is really funny over here. All of the infantry seem to think our work is very dangerous and they wouldn't go down one of our saps on a bet. Of course we wouldn't let any of them in as we keep all of our work to ourselves.

We have quite a few officers up at one time and so have to enlarge our sleeping quarters. We now have a dining-room or mess and above all a shower bath. Don't laugh because it is the truth. We put a barrel up on a stand and have a pipe with a spray leading from it and fill the barrel with water. I would hate like the mischief to have Fritz come over some fine morning if I were in it as it would be very embarrassing to say the least.

Back at rest at our billets we can plainly hear the rifle fire and machine-gun fire up the line. The flares go up all night and look fine. It is really very spectacular – all the different coloured lights going up and the flashes of shells bursting. It is not much fun I may say when right in it as it loses a lot of the charm. The next war I am going to get some job at a camp like that (Petawawa) and make sure it is really permanent. Don't you think it would be a wise stunt? It would save an awful lot of discomfort and I wouldn't be half scared to death so often.

I don't know whether I told you about our famous kitten. It is a cat with a history. There are a lot of trench cats and they are a blessing. You have no idea how thick and impudent the rats and mice are. Really and truly you sometimes have to kick a rat out of the way as he won't stir otherwise and there are some big fellows. To get back to our cat – it is called Whizz Bang. One of our men took pity on this kitten and brought it down here. It is very cute and lots of fun.

One of our officers had a fall off his motorcycle and hurt his knee badly. As a result of a couple of our officers being reported for speeding in a village, our privileges have been somewhat stopped and we have to go to the O.C. to get a motorcycle now. Flett has just come back from a short run and he had dinner with the Prince of Wales, some class eh? It was at some officers' club and the Prince happened to be there.

Love, Basil

Belgium, August 5/16

Dear Mother,

I have had quite a nice time since last I wrote you – we got up at six yesterday and went to a town about thirty miles from here to get some clothes. There is a beautiful park there and in the afternoon there was a band concert. It was awfully good but we missed the train home and stole a ride with some French privates on a freight train part of the way.

We have had a lot of excitement here lately and very interesting times. Did you know our company has been mentioned in dispatches? Our O.C. should get some decoration out of it. We were the means of saving a number of men's lives which is a whole lot – in brief, we gave warning of a mine and so kept the fellows from getting blown up.

Love, Basil

Aug. 14/16

Dear Mother,

I got several letters this morning. It surely was a coincidence, Ramsey and I meeting. I hope when he comes out here I shall be able to see him often.

We surely have a fine O.C., one of the best on the front. We got a wire from the Commander of the Canadian Corps congratulating the Company on work we did. That makes the second time we had distinguished the Company and it was through our half Company both times. It is much better up the line now when we hear far more of our shells going over to Fritz than he ever sends back. It is a much more comfortable feeling.

I will have been in France for six months tomorrow. It is a long time, isn't it? However, I have been mighty lucky so far. The harvest is on here now, all the fields are ripe and it surely looks funny seeing the people cutting their grain with a scythe.

I can't help thinking how really ugly the towns and villages in Canada are for the most part. They have none of this quaint look about them that the English and French villages have.

It is mighty decent of you to be so good to those fellows from Peta-wawa, and so long as you can do it, it is mighty good as they certainly appreciate it. I know that I long sometimes for someplace to go to when I feel a bit blue. It is all so cold-hearted out here. The winter is the worst and I still have memories of last February and March in the trenches, cold and sloppy and wet all the time. It is really very surprising the small amount of sickness there is. There is no fever at all scarcely. The men themselves realize the need of keeping the trenches as clean as possible and that helps a lot.

Don't worry about me, please. Everything is O.K.

Your loving son, Basil

Belgium, August 16/16

Dear Grace,

I am due up to the trenches tomorrow night and I wish I didn't have to go. There is no use feeling like that and I really don't mind once I get up there. We have been in France six months today and I guess we will be here for a while longer. I don't like the idea of another winter out here very much, but I never felt better than I do now and everything is going O.K.

Lots of love, Basil

August 16/16

Dear Father,

Our company has done some good work lately and a couple of our officers are likely to get something out of it. They surely deserve some recognition.

Some new men arrived in our company the other day and they are a fine looking bunch. We have a good bunch of men and they work hard. I think it is due to our O.C., Major North.

We can consider ourselves veterans now having been out here for six months. An officer the other day was up in the trenches looking for a friend where he was not supposed to be and got wounded. He would not go to the dressing-station but had us fix him up. Getting wounded under these circumstances is classed as self-inflicted wounds and you can be treated just as if you had wounded yourself.

The evenings lately have been wonderfully cool with a nice breeze and a bright moon. You can hardly realize there is a war on – it looks so quiet and peaceful.

Your loving son, Basil

Aug. 22/16

Dear Mother,

Ramsey, as you probably know, is out here now and I have seen him. He came over the night I came out of the trenches and was here for dinner. I did not get down until about 9 p.m. and he stayed around until about midnight and I took him home in the car.

Ramsey said that he had been living on Bully beef and hardtack for the couple of days before. A new outfit out here has to learn everything for themselves as things out here are different from what they expect as night is from day. A person has no idea what it is like unless he has seen it and lived in it himself. They are rather lucky getting out here now while summer is still here and so will get on to things a bit before winter comes.

Do you know, Mother, that on the 16th of next month we will be here in France for seven months. It is a long, long time when I look back on it. We, as a company, have been very lucky. I hope our luck sticks with us, but this is a game at which one cannot tell what is in store for us.

I was down at a show last night put on by one of the Imperial Divisions and it was really very good – all the latest popular songs. A small stage with acetylene lamps for footlights. The company consisted of five men and a pianist. The theatre was an old barn with a mud floor and the seats were long wooden benches, the whole surroundings being something like the shows we used to put on in Mrs. Lloyd's barn.

Your loving son, Basil

Aug. 24/16

Dear Mother,

I think that I have written to you already this time down, but in case I may have overlooked it, I will write a short note now. I usually make a point of writing to you the first day down.

Major Melianis, my old company commander in the 59th has been killed. I was awfully sorry to see it as he is an awfully nice man and left a family. Major McLaren has been wounded too. They have only been out here a couple of weeks and I have been out now between six and seven months and have not been scratched as yet.

I have seen Ramsey several times lately. He is camped within about
five miles of us so I have seen him quite often. It is mighty nice to have
someplace to go like that to see someone.

With love, Basil

Aug. 25/16

Dear Grace,

I am feeling pretty rotten now having been under the weather all day.
There are quite a few lately feeling sick, owing I think to the water.

We had very bad luck last night. Do you remember Simpson, the
Scotchman who was on the train with us going to St. John? Well the
poor chap was killed last night. We lost him and three men killed and six
wounded all by one small shell. Of all the rotten luck, that is the worst.
These things have to happen but I was awfully sorry about Simpson.
Things go on the same as usual and I suppose the incident will soon be
closed.

I saw Ramsey again today before I came up here and he looks fine. It
was great to see him again.

I wish I could get back home for a while. It is a long time since I have
been there and very probably will be a long time again before I will be
able to see it. Although we have the upper hand now Fritzy has an awful
lot of fight left in him.

Lots of love, Basil

Aug. 29/16

Dear Mother,

At present, it is raining cats and dogs. It surely will make the roads
into rotten shape and the trenches will be fierce. Thank goodness I am
not up the line and I surely pity the poor beggars who are. They will
have to crawl into their miserable dugouts and haven't much chance to
get dry once they are wet. There has been quite a straffe on all day today
and the big guns are all going pretty lively. When they start firing the
whole place shakes.

I think I told you about Simpson being killed. I was very sorry about
it. Anyway it was sudden and he did not suffer. He always dreaded the
thought of being smashed up and living for a while. I feel pretty badly
over it as he was an awfully good friend to me.

Several of our officers are pretty sick now. Flett has gone to hospital and Bob Murray has a severe attack of dysentry. I have tried my hardest to get typhoid fever or pneumonia and get a Blightie out of it but I can't seem to do it no how.

I am all OK at present and feel fine.

Love, Basil

Aug. 31/16

Dear Grace,

Lunch won't be ready for a while so I am taking advantage of the wait by writing to you. It is a lovely day today after the last couple of days which have been fierce. It rained almost steadily for nearly a week but today the sun is out bright and it makes a chap feel like living. I saw Ramsey yesterday for about two minutes. I went over to their camp but they had fallen in to go to the trenches for a while so I had only a very few minutes to see him.

Captain Spencer who is in charge of our half-company has been given the Military Cross. He surely deserved it and I am glad he has got it. He got it for a stunt on our front for which the company was congratulated by the Corps commander.

Our work has interesting episodes but no one knows about them as the work has to be kept secret. It is rather exciting at times underground. You get so close you can hear the Huns talking.

Love, Basil

Sept. 8/16

Dear Mother,

It will be three months ago tomorrow since I went on leave to London. It doesn't seem that long but it really is three whole months. However, leave for tunnelling [companys] has opened up again and there are not very many ahead of me.

We had a spell of nearly a whole week of steady rain but everything has dried up again. I was out yesterday on my motorbike trying to look Ramsey up but his battalion is up in the line and I did not see him. However, on my way home I passed the Guelph battery on the move and it was great to see the fellows again. I saw Lornie Biggs, McCarthy and White McDonald [friends from Pembroke]. I knew one of the officers in it too, having gone through a couple of years at S.P.S. with him.

Colonel Dawson [of the 59th] is over here now too, in Command of a battalion. He came over here to see me, but I was up in the trenches at the time. I have not had a chance to look him up since, either.

I have to trouble you again to send me a couple of tins of seal oil, I think it is, for the boots. It is very hard to get good boot oil over here. You can get this oil at Fraser's shoe store. I shall soon have to wear my big boots again steadily as the winter rain will be on us in another month or so.

Old McCue is still with us. He often comes up for a chat and I never see him but he says, 'I wish I were back in Pembroke and driving that cutter up to your father's door.' He is quite a case and goes on a spree every once in a while. He was up for office again this morning.

Major North goes on leave next and is feeling pretty good over it. He certainly is a prince and is the best O.C. along this line.

I had a letter from Grandmother yesterday and was very glad indeed to hear from her. I must write to her soon again.

Love, Basil

Sept. 8/16

Dear Grace,

I go up the line again tomorrow night for another tour but I have no real dislike for it this time like I had for a week or two. I guess this is because leave is in view again. I should have my leave in a little less than two months. That really is not terribly long you know. I don't suppose I shall have as good a time this time over in Blightie as I did last, as Ramsey won't be there. I wish that you could be over there at that time and we could have a really good time of it. However, there is no use of wishing for the moon. I certainly am going to try my best to dodge all the shells coming my way between now and the time when my leave comes.

Love, Basil

Sept. 14/16

Dear Mother,

It is raining cats and dogs today and I am sitting in the mess beside a grate fire. Perhaps from this you will think this is a luxurious life. The trouble is we cannot get very much coke and no firewood so the fire is not much to talk about. However, it is better than nothing.

Last night, I came down from the trenches and slept in pretty late this morning. When I got up the mail had come in and there was a letter from you. I had been wondering who was sending me Saturday Night and now I know and will write Mrs. Williams to thank her.

Last night was a beautiful night – bright moonlight. Our camp is on the top of a small rise and from here we get a good view. We can see from here right to the ridge that the Germans are on which is about six or seven miles away.

There was a band concert last night just far enough away to soften the music and when a popular song was played, I could hear faintly the men singing. It did not sound a bit like war, and if it hadn't been for the flares going up and the intermittent machine-gun fire, I could have thought myself back home in Canada. All evening and well into the morning the transport rumbles by on the main road up to the trenches. There is every sort of vehicle, motor lorries, G.S. [General Service] wagons, gigs, limbers, motor cars and occasionally a motorcycle. I do not exaggerate when I say that for nearly four hours every night there is a steady stream of transport going up and then they all come back empty. When you think of all this stuff, material for the engineers, rations and ammunition, all going up every night and particularly no loads coming back, it is stupendous.

About that piece of work of ours, I wrote about before, Capt. Spencer got the MC for it. Bob Murray deserves a lot of credit for it too. I was not in on it, although I was right up there when it happened. After the Germans blew their mine, a week or so after our men captured a piece of German gallery and have things now so that the Germans cannot move in the mining end very much. There is an opening here for promotion, not an extra star but a better job and I am in line for it but there is no chance of me getting it. The reason for this is mostly my age.

I am glad you are having those fellows from the Camp up to the house as often as you do. They certainly appreciate it and will remember it.

I went over to try to see Ramsey this afternoon, but he is in the trenches. I think they are relieved tonight so I should see him tomorrow. They will be only a little over a mile from our camp when they come out to rest.

Lots of love, Basil

22/9/16

Dear Father,

I have not written to you for quite a while but I will make up for it now. You must take off your hat to No. 1 Tunnelling Coy. There was a competition the other day for all the tunnelling companies working in blue clay and about ten companies sent in teams. We won out and had about eight inches over the ones closest to us. No. 3 Canadians were second. We beat out the Imperial companies and Australian companies so you see there are no flies on us. It surely tickled us, especially as one of the Imperial Companies a month or two ago, sent up some men to show us how to do it. Once our fellows learned how to 'kick' they certainly made the dust fly. Of course, mining we cannot use picks as it makes too much noise and we do what is called 'kicking.' It is faster than picking and much quieter. It is very eerie having to whisper and move very quietly when under ground, but I like it very much indeed. Sharp and I were doing some surveying the other day. It was fine to get using a transit again. It is much more interesting than ordinary working that way as we never know over here when we will have to duck.

Love, Basil

22/9/16

Dear Grace,

I feel very lazy today and you must not mind if this letter is rather disconnected, but I cannot keep my thoughts together very well.

We are having lovely sunny days again after a spell of wet weather. It was really rotten during our last turn up the line because there was so much mud everywhere and it rained all the time nearly.

I saw Ramsey yesterday afternoon. I just struck him by chance and he and Bob Murray and myself went into one of the towns and had tea. We then had our pictures taken together and if it is any good, I will send you a copy of it. I expect Ramsey over this evening for dinner. I expect that he will be moving away from here pretty soon and I will be mighty sorry as it is great to see him once in a while. They have been in the trenches pretty much most of the time here so that I have not seen him very often, but have seen him at every opportunity.

I saw the picture of Pembroke Needle Battalion today in an issue of the Montreal Daily Standard. It was a very good picture and it is an awfully good picture of Mother. It surely was great to see all those faces again that I knew quite well.

Love, Basil

France, 23/9/16

Dear Mother,

I was surprised today to say the least to see, when I picked up the Montreal Standard, your face. I can tell you it gave me a pang of lonesomeness. It was in a picture of the needle battalion at work in the town hall.

I saw Ramsey yesterday afternoon for a while and expected him to come over here for dinner tonight, but I guess he could not get away. They are moving away from this section soon and I hate to see them go as they will be in a pretty warm spot I guess. Honestly, I would rather see Ramsey back in England and let me take his place. I sort of feel mean because our job is much softer than his. It is nicer work, we have more comforts and it is not as risky. I wish he were going to be around here too for a while longer because it is fine to be able to see him once in a while. I guess from now on I won't be able to see him at all. However, it cannot be helped and there is no use worrying.

Things have dried up here a whole lot which makes it a lot more like a civilized country. Last week here was fierce. It rained steadily for a week with the result that the mud got churned up and was about a foot deep in places. It was nothing at all though to what it will be this winter when it will rain all the time and the mud will be mighty bad. I don't think that we are very likely to move away from this front for quite a while and I am getting rather fed up on the place, but I don't think we would be as comfortable in another place as we are here. One of our officers, Brown by name, has gone back to Canada on two months sick leave. He is a lucky devil and I would like to be in his shoes. Jeffery is back with us now and seems tickled to death to get back here. He has been down at the base for several months and got pretty well fed up on it.

The line up here is very quiet and there is hardly any shelling at all. It is just like home.

That picture today made me feel homesick. I don't know why but I think it was you working at the table because it looked so awfully natural, and it was such a surprise besides.

Lots of love, Basil

24/9/16

Dear Mother,

I was very disappointed today as I expected to see Ramsey again before he left this section, but I could not locate him as he had left before he could get leave to come over here. I saw him the day before yesterday however, and it was not as if I hadn't seen him at all. I certainly am sorry that he has left this section.

My leave is getting mighty close now. I go four weeks from tomorrow if luck is with me.

Up on the wall of our mess we have some old bones of some old animal which was dug up out of the blue clay about forty feet under ground. They must belong to some old prehistoric animal and are very large – too large for any present-day animal.

I am going off on a little jaunt tomorrow on the lorrie to get some material. It will be quite a change as I have not been away from the camp for some time now. I get spells once in a while of feeling terribly fed up on this whole life and I feel somewhat that way now, although it does not do much good.

I go up to the line tomorrow.

Lots of love, Basil

30/9/16

Dear Mother,

This is only a short letter but it is late. The main part of this letter is a request that you cable to the Bank of Montreal, Waterloo Place, London, the sum of fifteen pounds to my credit. This is to be taken from my assigned pay at home. I am going on leave in three weeks from the day after tomorrow, that is Oct. 23rd. I have to get a new uniform and several other things and so will need extra money. As leave only comes once in four months, I have no intention of stinting myself a great deal while over there.

I said in a letter a while ago that I thought I would try for a safety-first job in Blightie but on thinking it over carefully, I have come to the conclusion that I don't really think it would be right for me to do that. I started out in this show with this company and I would like to see it through with them if I am lucky enough. Don't you think that is a sensible view? Why should I look for a job like that? There are lots out here a whole lot worse off than I am and if they stick it so can I.

Lots of love, Basil

In the trenches, 6/10/16

Dear Father,

I received your letter this afternoon. Capt. Spencer brought several up and yours was among them. I am glad that you are all working towards conscription back home as it will catch a bunch of those slackers around home and I guess there are a lot everywhere. I am glad Desmond [a cousin from Pembroke] is in the artillery and he deserves credit going in as a private. They don't have it nearly as hard as the infantry do over here as they have practically none of the trench work to do.

Bob Murray was relieved this afternoon and he surely was tickled to get down. He goes on leave on Monday and is glad to get away. I shall pretty soon follow him. The only thing that I am sorry for is that Ramsey won't be over there with me.

Your loving son, Basil

9/10/16

Dear Grace,

Today is a wonderful day here and a very welcome change. We can see for miles right up to the line. It is very quiet for a bright sunny day and I am surprised as usually the guns are at least ranging on sunny days.

This month is surely going fast. I can hardly realize that eight months have passed since we first landed in France. You know we are now camped only a matter of a couple of hundred yards from the spot we came to first for instruction. We were only here for a week at that time, but we have been in this camp now since last May sometime. The camp is splendid, nice and comfortable. We are getting our dugout fixed up pretty well up the line. There is nothing like being as comfortable as possible under the circumstances, is there?

Bob Murray is away on leave at present and I will be there in less than two weeks now myself, and hope to see Ramsey in London by good luck. At present he is in Manchester Hospital with his eyes. He is a lucky beggar in a way but I don't suppose that he sees it that way.

Tonight is a beautiful warm light night with a steady breeze blowing towards Fritz. There are practically no flares going up as it is so bright and the wind blowing away from us we can hear no machine guns and standing outside it is mighty hard to imagine that there is a war on at all.

I go up the line tomorrow and I guess that I will then be able to realize quite fully that there is a war on alright.

                                        Your loving brother, Basil

P.S. I received your parcel alright containing tobacco and shortbread. Write soon and often. B.

7 ✻ Reunion ✻ ✻ ✻ ✻ ✻ ✻ ✻ ✻ ✻ ✻

Basil had been at the front for almost six months when Ramsey finally arrived in France – despite our father's intention that his eldest son should be the first to get overseas. The 38th Battalion had left Bermuda in June, and after a month or so in England they had reached the battle-line early in August.

Ramsey had one of the most difficult and dangerous jobs at the front. As a lieutenant in the infantry, he was required to lead his platoon during attacks over the top of the trenches in the face of enemy fire; in the front-line dugouts and trenches he was constantly exposed to snipers and machine-gun fire as well as bursting shells of various kinds. Basil always worried about his brother, for he knew his chances for survival in such a position were comparatively slim.

Unlike the Tunnellers, who tended to stay in one spot on the line, the infantrymen were moved around to where they were needed. In the beginning, however, Ramsey happened to be stationed fairly close to Basil. His letters home described his early impressions of the war.

August 18, 1916

Dear Grace,

We are in dugouts now – or really not dugouts – they are built up. The architecture is rather pretty from the front. I went out and looked at them this morning but we are supposed to stay inside most of the time. We are not in the front line and it is very peaceful here. Our own batteries make a row every little while but there is hardly any reply at all. A couple of our dugouts are wrecked by shells and the ground around in spots looks like a crokonole(?) board (or one of those boards you play a game with marbles on) but the Germans when they try for a thing appear to miss quite accurately and regularly. They appear to hit towns all right; one we came through en route here was only a skeleton.

Machine guns were going in good trim last night. We slept like a lot of tops, at least I did and when I rolled out at daybreak I felt great. Nearly everybody else was snoring but I got shaved and cleaned up. We didn't bring much water but did the trick with our water bottles and some tried very unsanitary mud puddles. All our men shaved and cleaned their equipment. Our men wanted to roam around the country a little today but·they are a fairly reasonable lot and do pretty well what they are told.

There is a sand-bag Y.M.C.A. not very far away and we can get truck to eat and papers by sending out an orderly. The Y.M.C.A.'s over here are all to the good as far as I have seen them up to date. We saw one dandy aerial combat yesterday. It was rather rotten coming up here stumbling over shell craters etc. but these craters aren't very deep like you read about, 2 or 4 feet deep and 8 or 10 feet diameter is the ordinary run and smaller if it is on a hard road bed.

We are a little bored today. Our experience is new and that keeps us from getting very weary with sticking around like a lot of warts. We will probably get up in the front line (we are in the front line system but not the front line trench) before very long. Just this moment a real picnic has started. Our people are having a great time and are loud about it. The other people may decide to reply in a minute or two. I got your letter yesterday and it was good you did so very well at tennis in Cobalt. I remain your loving brother.

Ramsey

Trenches, Sept. 4/16

Dear Grace,

This is really the first opportunity I have had to write for a little time. I got your letter a day or two ago and like to get a letter like that telling about the little things around Pembroke and your trip up the Ottawa. We had a couple of bombardments since we came here. They are pretty well rotten. You don't mind the bullets so much. It is the trench mortars that get my goat properly. I had one narrow call and don't particularly want any more sausages my way.

Tell mother not to worry very much about anybody out here. You make up your mind pretty well to it and old timers out here get pretty well calloused. Our trenches aren't bad at all and will probably be better later and our tours of duty are not too long.

You can get lots of truck to buy in little villages back of the line but you can't get any of that good candy like mother makes.

It is raining now a little bit and will probably be muddy up in front, but here's hoping there will be no sausages.

Love to everybody,

Ramsey

September 8/16

Dear Grace,

I am writing this in the gloomy shadows of a big room. The tapestried walls are a bit dilapidated, torn in spots; the deep red curtains on the windows are soiled; the fireplace lacks a fire; but all this is sunk in deep shadow and shows up little. The large oak table in the centre of the room with a solitary candle is the one bright spot and, with this paper spread out in front of me and my back reclining against the luxurious springiness of a settee, I am quite ready to write you a reasonably long letter.

Our beds, varying from a large four-poster to a temporary contrivance of canvas, are ranged in the deepest shadows along one end of the room. Last night, sleeping here after a fairly long spell in the trenches, I dreamed of an endless procession of people with sandbags going by the end of my bed and also of the count or 'Graf' or somebody who formerly owned this chateau. It was a curious dream altogether. I could easily dream of ghosts and things.

There are all kinds of rooms in this chateau. The window-panes are mostly broken. The rooms are pretty bare but strangely enough, the place is full of mirrors and none of them are broken – large pier glasses, round mirrors, square mirrors face you at every turn. The wine cellar which we visited today is quite empty. We were told a lot of rooms underground existed but we could only find one complete floor. This building is quite large – not immense – but bigger than anything in Pembroke and runs up to quite a height in pinnacles etc. It is completely surrounded by a moat, and quite an interesting lot of grounds, formally laid out. I went for a swim in the moat tonight – it was pretty cold but very invigorating. All the out-buildings are shelled to bits. I went to a town today that was quite O.K. We had an O.K. lunch. I got a little truck I wanted and we walked a good part of the way back; it had not been shelled at all at any time and was good to get into.

I would like to write a lot more but will turn in.

Love to everybody at home and yourself very much.

Your loving brother, Ramsey.

Belgium
September 10, 1916.

Dear Grace,

I just wrote a letter to Mr. J.T. Lamb, an old dodger on St. David's I. He told me before I left there he would forward some lily bulbs to Pembroke. Next January or sometime around then – you can keep a lookout for them. He will undoubtedly send them. He is an old partly colored fisherman that used to row me across from St. Georges at nights any time I wanted to come over late and was a very good old sort indeed.

We are still in our chateau – it's a little tiresome sticking around here doing practically nothing. Our men do working parties and things but we will all get lots of work to do when we go back to our rest camp. You get a little row around here when the guns open up but often it's so quiet it fairly gets on your nerves. We had a false alarm here the other night – the gas alarm went and everybody had to go up to the front line trenches in the middle of the night but nothing happened. Our own guns made an awful uproar for quite a time however.

Love, your loving brother,
Ramsey

The 'narrow call' Ramsey mentioned casually in his letter of September 4 had been a good deal more dramatic than he had described it, and had consequences even he could not have imagined at the time. He had been sitting, as he later told us, between two of his men in the trench outside their dugout when a 'sausage,' a powerful bomb lobbed over from the German line, had exploded beside them. Both the other men were killed; Ramsey's uniform had been torn, but he seems to have been protected from the blast by their bodies. Although physically unharmed, he was emotionally damaged; in fact, he was suffering from severe shell-shock.

While staying at the chateau behind the lines a few days later, he had bad dreams at night, and his nerves were shattered to the extent that on his next round of duty in the front-line trench he had great difficulty in forcing himself to enter the communication trenches.

Worst of all, his eyes had been affected and he was gradually but steadily going blind. The seriousness of his condition was discovered by his commanding officer as his regiment was being marched to the Somme to take part in one of the great battles there. Ramsey failed to salute his colonel because he could not see him. Because of this blindness, which fortunately turned out to be temporary, he was given sick leave and sent to a hospital in England to recover. He wrote to me from Manchester early in October.

Oct. 5th 1916

Dear Grace,

I trust you will be able to make this out without too much strain to your eyes and your imagination. I can write all right if you aren't too particular about the way I do it. They stick drops of Atropene? in my eyes that keeps them in pretty rotten shape for seeing things. I go out in the afternoon and walk or have tea or something but can't read anything at all and it's funny what an awful difference it makes in the ordinary things of life. Manchester is a pretty rotten town. It is bigger than any town in Canada (800,000) but Toronto or Montreal have it over it like a tent. There are lots of warehouses, factories, docks and a ship canal etc. but its very smoky and dirty, no imposing buildings – nothing at all in fact. There are half a dozen towns in Canada with a better looking shopping district and there is only one really big first class hotel here and about four or so theatres. I can't go to a show but think I will take one in just for fun. I can hear it anyway. We can go out 2-6 each day. Write anytime you can. Thanks awfully for the O.K. parcel I got just before I left France – maple sugar, handkerchiefs etc. It was all to the good. In going through my truck the other — I ran into a letter I wrote when we were at Kemmel Chateau. I removed the envelope and will stick — in with this just to show I really did write. I don't know how I did not mail it.

Much love Y.L. brother, Ramsey

P.S. Basil will probably get leave in a couple or three weeks.

When news reached us that Ramsey was in hospital at Manchester, threatened with blindness, it caused consternation. My parents were able to accept the situation when I announced my plans to go to England as soon as possible to be with him. In reply to my cable 'Do you want me to come?' Ramsey had wired 'Please come.'

After a few days of consideration my mother decided to accompany me. When they heard of our venture, Welland's mother, Mrs Williams, and her sister Ada Dickson agreed to come along as well. We needed only passports in order to make the trip, and we obtained these easily from Ottawa within the week. Within ten days we were all on board the Canadian Pacific liner *Missanabie*, sister ship of the *Metagama* on which Basil had sailed at the beginning of the year, bound for England from Montreal.

For me it was an exciting first trip across the Atlantic. But there were dangers as well. In May of the previous year the Cunard liner *Lusitania* had been sunk off the British Isles by a German submarine with the loss of over a thousand lives. Passenger liners were still going back and forth in late 1916, but some of them were known to be carrying troops and therefore liable to enemy attack. The *Missanabie* was itself torpedoed towards the end of the war.

The ship was very crowded, another sailing having just been cancelled. The four of us had to share a modest stateroom and, to add to the discomfort, the sea was very rough. The majority of the passengers were women and children, the families of men in the Canadian forces who had connections in the British Isles, many having been born there. The only 'military' on board was a group of young men in civilian clothes who were going to England to be trained in the Royal Flying Corps. They made life interesting for some young women I knew, who came to my cabin each day begging me to join them and play the piano; when I remained in my berth they borrowed my music and even some of my clothes. I was too seasick to care.

On reaching the Irish Sea, where submarines were successfully sinking many ships, our lifeboats were swung out on davits ready for a quick abandonment of the ship. This proved unnecessary as a great storm was raging which made it difficult for the enemy 'subs' to operate. Some of the lifeboats were blown away. The captain ordered the passengers to remain in the lounges and listen for the siren. The order was obeyed by all except the very seasick, including me, who remained in their berths and wished the ship would sink.

On landing at Liverpool the nightmare of the voyage quickly faded. There at the dock to meet us was a fine-looking soldier. Ramsey had just been released from hospital to spend a long sick leave while his blindness gradually vanished as he recovered from shell-shock. With our mother, we now travelled to London where we would stay until Basil would have leave from the front and could join us.

We found London crowded with thousands of men from all over the Empire, on leave from the front line in France and Flanders, from army training camps, and from the navy. It was a very exciting place to be.

In Westminster Abbey we found Wolfe's tomb draped with the colours of all the Canadian battalions, a brilliant spot in all the surrounding greyness. One day we attended a remarkable concert there when the famous Sheffield Choir, accompanied by a symphony orchestra, sang *Elijah* for the overseas wounded. The great nave was a sea of blue hospital uniforms interspersed with the veils of the nursing sisters, and, as we sat in a side aisle behind great columns, we were deeply stirred by the beauty and tragedy of the scene. We explored the royal chapels and found them beautiful though sandbags covered the ancient tombs. It gave us a special thrill in London to come upon things unexpectedly that we had known about for a long time, such as finding a gothic arch in an ugly brick wall in Smithsfield Markets, which led to the ancient Norman church of Saint Bartholomew, and coming suddenly upon the dingy Guild Hall tucked away in a narrow street. We were delighted to find ourselves one day at Amen Corner. That was not far from St Paul's Cathedral, where we attended a service one Sunday morning: among the hundreds of men in the uniforms of New Zealand, Australia, and Canada, near us sat four Indians from the Golden Lake Reserve not far from Pembroke.

Sometimes, as we walked about London, I found it necessary to act as a sort of bodyguard for my handsome brother. The streets seemed to be awash with eager females anxious to comfort lonely soldiers. The theatres, as always, had splendid shows. They were crowded with men in uniform who could enjoy themselves there in contrast to the large hotels where only those wearing mufti, or civilian clothes, were allowed to dance. A favourite musical show was *Chu Chin Chow*; everywhere one heard the 'hit' song from it, 'Anytime's Kissing Time.' Favourite plays were *Romance*, in which Doris Keane was involved in an illicit love affair with a clergyman, which I thought very romantic but Ramsey felt was slightly immoral, and *London Pride*, a play set in a dugout in France: the theme was the pride a young officer felt when he discovered that a fellow officer serving in his unit in the trenches was the champion rugby player of England.

Not far from London at Virginia Water in Windsor Great Park was an installation of the Canadian Forestry Corps. This was a very Canadian outfit, under the command of General Alex McDougall of Ottawa, organized to provide timber for use by the army. Their forestry operations and Canadian-type sawmills were set up in Scotland and France as well as in Windsor Great Park. This operation was of great interest to the King, who frequently dropped in for tea at the officers' mess when he was staying at Windsor. With our mother, we were included in a party arranged by Colonel G.V. White to visit the installation and have tea. To us, coming from the Ottawa Valley, the shriek of saws cutting through logs was a familiar sound indeed.

When Ramsey heard that his battalion had suffered heavy casualties in the Battle of the Somme, he tried to discover how his friends had fared, especially the men of his platoon, but it was difficult to locate any in hospital in London without their regimental numbers. We were able to find some of his officer friends, however, and visited them.

Meanwhile, Basil, who had had leave late in October and had visited Ramsey in Manchester, had returned to the front, not knowing that my mother and I were on our way to England. The letters he sent to us continued to go to Canada, and he was naturally disappointed when he learned that he had missed us.

6/11/16

Dear Ramsey,

I am back up in the trenches again and the mud is damnable. I slip and slide all over the place but have been lucky enough so far not to fall into a shell hole – they of course are all chuck full of water.

I had a very nice trip back. I stayed in London and slept one night at Dr. Stewart's. Went to see a nurse that Bob Murray told me to see. Say, Ramsey, she is one of the nicest girls I have seen in a long, long time and I wish I could have seen more of her. She is a real peach, good looking and lots of fun.

There was an awful pile of mail for me when I got back and I have been reading it in installments.

I hope you get a good leave out of this sickness – good luck.

Your loving brother, Basil

France 11/11/16

Dear Father,

I have not written to you for some time so tonight I am scribbling off a short note to you.

Everything is going fine with us. There is lots of rain and mud but we get accustomed to them in time. Christmas is drawing near once more so we are beginning to prepare for it. We are ordering a bunch of turkeys from England and nuts, raisins, etc., in fact, nearly all the things that go with Christmas.

I had a splendid time on leave, but have told Grace about it in her letter so won't repeat it here.

Your loving son, Basil

France 11/11/16

Dear Grace,

I am back in this 'lovely sunny France' (?) once more. There is lots and lots and lots of mud everywhere and I'll swear that if I haven't already eaten my allotted peck of dirt, I have done so this week. I have mud for breakfast, lunch and dinner, with a little extra thrown in for supper at night.

We have had a lot of excitement here this week and it has been lots of fun. I can't tell you about it but it was very exciting for sure. There is a bit more shelling now than there used to be, but it is nothing like what it was when we first came up to this part of the world.

I surely was surprised to hear about Desmond and wasn't he a silly ass. I don't think a chap should get married like that before coming over here. However, it was just like a stunt that he would pull off and I bet she was a good looking girl. You needn't worry about me slipping anything like that over on you for a while yet. Don't lose any sleep over it. I haven't seen any girls since I left Canada that affected me enough to do the Romeo stunt with although I met some rather nice girls when I was on leave. I really had a fine time.

Dr. and Mrs. Ollershaw in Manchester were really awfully decent to me and have asked me to spend my next leave with them. In fact, I have four invitations to spend my next leave with people. I saw Dr. and Mrs. Gray in London and Mrs. Gray asked me to go there next time. Dr. and Mrs. Stewart were very decent too. I stayed two days with them on the way back. They live in Surbiton. Dr. Stewart is a brother of Jack Hope's partner and Mrs. Stewart, who was Miss Gooderham, is awfully nice. She has adopted me as her son she says when over here. I also saw Mrs. White. They asked me to stay there next time too. I saw Alex McDougall who is now Brigadier of the Forestry Brigade and on the General Staff. He'll be one of those Red Jaks soon I guess. He is a great character and I surely like him. I saw Kenneth [McDougall] when over there too and he has his three stars up. Blightie jobs are the place for promotion believe me. The poor beggars out here very seldom get it at all.

Your loving brother, Basil

13/11/16

Dear Mother,

I had a little holiday yesterday and today and it is fine getting away from the camp for a while. The lorrie had to come down here to the coast for some material and the adjutant sent me with it, so here I am. We got down here about two o'clock yesterday afternoon and I am leaving this morning about ten. Bill Hardy who is going on leave came down with me so that we fooled around here together. We were out to see a couple of French girls last night that one of our chaps knew when down here at hospital and we had not a bad time. They could speak English fairly well so we got along jake. One of them could play and sing very well so that it was something like getting back home. It is very funny hearing them sing English songs especially the rags.

We are staying at the Officers' Club which is a very comfortable place and serve very good meals. In fact, we had roast chicken at dinner last night. It was almost worth an eighty mile ride in a lorrie for the meals alone.

I am writing this at 8 a.m. while waiting for Bill Hardy to come down for breakfast. I have to beat it out to the R.E. park right after breakfast for the load I take back and then will very likely leave about ten this morning.

I have just met a chap I went through varsity with and was glad to see him. It surely is nice to run across them over here and they are everywhere.

Your loving son, Basil

14/11/16

Dear Ramsey,

I received your letter yesterday and am mighty glad to hear from you. You should have a good time on leave and be sure and make the most of it. With regard to that transfer of mine, I find there is a lot of red tape in connection with it and it will take much longer than I expected. In fact, it probably may take six or eight weeks yet before it will go through. It will not be a transfer, but will likely be 'attached for duty.' Later, I intend to try to get into the Canadian wing which is now being formed. They did not try to stop me here from going because there is an order out against that, but they all say I am foolish as needless to say the casualties in the R.F.C. are higher than in our unit. However, it is a good branch of the service and I hope that I can get into it.

As it will take some time before I can get into the R.F.C. and then have to spend three months out here with them, it will be quite a while before I shall be back in Blighty again.

Your loving brother, Basil

Basil had confided to Ramsey what he had not yet told the rest of us: that he was applying for a transfer into the Royal Flying Corps. By this time he had learned that my mother and I were in England, and he was determined to see us before we returned home.

19/11/16

Dear Father,

I had letters yesterday from Mother, Grace and from you. From the letters, Mother and Grace are in England now, and just to think that I came back from England about two weeks ago. It was rotten luck, wasn't it, that I couldn't be there when they are there. I haven't heard from Mother or Grace yet but should very soon. I think they might get over to France at the coast for a few days and I could probably get down there for a few days when out resting. However, it is out of the question for me to think of getting over to Blighty at all.

The weather is bloody awful over here now and if it is like this all winter, it will be fierce. However, we Canadians can stand it, I guess, better than the Australians who are used to hot weather. They certainly find it pretty tough over here. The other day we had a fire going in our dugout up the line. The chimney goes up through the earth and comes out beside a communication trench. Some poor mut, seeing the smoke coming out, put a full sand-bag on the top with the result that we were smoked out down below in about one minute.

I came down from the trenches last night. The O.C. has just told me he will try and get me a few days leave in Blightie soon. It is mighty decent of him, isn't it? Especially as I have come back from leave only two weeks ago.

Today is awfully bleak out and it is very cold. It really is terribly depressing and I feel mighty sorry for those poor infantrymen in the line these nights.

I hope you aren't lonesome at home alone.

Love, Basil

22/11/16

My dear Mother,

I received your letter this morning and was very glad indeed to hear from you. I am sorry you had such a rough trip across. About me seeing you, I don't think that it is possible for me to get leave to England although I might work it. The best I can do would be a week-end leave. I am going to see you for sure somehow even if I have to desert.

I am off up the line tonight for four days. I did not know you had any idea of coming over or I most certainly would have let you know I was going over on leave.

Love, Basil

22/11/16

Dear Mother,

In a rush – leaving for trenches right away. Latest news – the O.C. thinks he can get me a few days leave.

Love, Basil

24/11/16

Dear Grace,

Just got your letter. There surely was a war on here this afternoon – all afternoon – and things were pretty lively. I hope it won't be like this steady, because if it is we will have rather a rough time of it.

I certainly am going to do all in my power to get special leave to see you. Major North is trying to get it for me which I think is mighty decent seeing I only got back from leave three weeks ago.

Love, Basil

25/11/16

Dear Mother,

Just a few lines while I am not busy. At present I am in my dugout. Bob Murray and several others are here and the gramophone is going.

I wish you would please go and call on Mrs. Stewart in Surbiton. She and Dr. Stewart were awfully decent to me when I was in England. I know you would like them both.

Love, Basil

One evening early in December Basil arrived at our hotel in Bedford Square. A group of people were chatting beside the fire in the reception room after dinner and I had joined them. I became aware that a soldier was standing in the darkened hall, smiling quietly, with tousled hair, a haversack on his back. A rush and a hug and I quickly led him to our mother's room. Ramsey was there and the reunion for all of us was an ecstatic occasion. It was as if he had come back from the dead.

First he must remove some of the mud and grime from the trenches. He opened the haversack he had been carrying and was amazed to discover a collection of ferocious-looking war souvenirs; obviously he had picked up the wrong haversack on the channel boat. There was a cudgel studded with nails, a leather thong to slip over the wrist, useful for trench raids, and, the most frightening object, a very large grenade equipped with a wooden handle and streamers. Ramsey, an expert in such things, thought the grenade might not be detonated. The question was how to dispose of this dangerous object. We went out into the darkened streets to find the Thames River, but better than that, after wandering for a while, we found a London 'Bobbie.' He was not overjoyed with the present we gave him but decided it was his duty to take it. Returning to the hotel we were joined by our mother and set out to find a restaurant with good food and music.

Carefully we planned Basil's precious eight-day leave. We decided to go by train to Scotland, the home of our ancestors, which proved to be a perfect place for a holiday. We stayed in Edinburgh at the Caledonian Hotel, which was then in its hey-day, in rooms that looked across the park to the castle on the hill. It was all we had hoped for: the romantic castle, the beautiful park, the ancient streets leading to Holyrood Palace with its bloody history, the shops with familiar Scottish names. We felt at home.

In the Caledonian Hotel beauty and gaiety reigned. The battle fleet was in the Forth and so the dinner hour was a scene of elegance with the handsome uniforms of the naval officers and the lovely gowns and jewels of their wives. Compared with London the food was lavish. Probably because officers in the uniform of Canada were unusual there and so attracted their attention, several naval officers invited Ramsey and Basil to visit the fleet with them. They felt this was an invitation not to be missed, even though in the midst of a war naval vessels could sail suddenly without a moment's warning. They were put ashore in time, but they wondered, if they had been taken to sea, whether or not they would have been court-martialed for being 'absent without leave.'

One day we travelled to Stirling. Looking from the battlements of the castle towards Bannockburn and recalling the famous battle, we felt our Scottish blood stirring, though several generations had passed since our ancestors had crossed the sea. As children we had delighted in stories of the Middle Ages, and now, being alone on the battlements, we amused ourselves playing the parts of ancient warriors, thus forgetting for a little while the war that had brought us all across the Atlantic. As we were leaving to catch our train back to Edinburgh, Basil stopped for a moment to look at an ancient tomb. There lay the effigy of a knight with crossed legs showing that he had been to the Crusades. He stooped to read the inscription and a chilling shadow seemed to pass as he looked up and said: 'Perhaps he is the parfait gentle knight that Chaucer wrote about. He was only twenty-five.'

We travelled back to London by a day train and spent the night in our hotel. Our mother did not sleep that night and wakened us early in the morning. It was raining heavily and with difficulty we secured a horse-drawn cab to take us to the station. As we passed Buckingham Palace we noticed that many rooms were lighted and we wondered if the King got up so early. There were bright lights too in Victoria Station, and much confusion as soldiers rushed to have papers signed before boarding the 'leave' train for the channel port. Basil secured a place in the dining-car for breakfast, then came to the end of the car to wave goodbye. We watched with sadness as the train pulled slowly away, and our one thought was 'Would we ever see him again?'

It was now December and a few days before Christmas Ramsey received orders to be ready to rejoin his battalion. He was to proceed to the base at Shorncliffe in the south of England at the beginning of the year. On his way back to the front he sent me the following letter.

Jan. 6/17

Dear Little Sister,

I am in a town in France and therefore not in the trenches yet. They dumped us off here this a.m. and we don't start again till this afternoon sometime, so you see they treat us fairly well, taking us up to the front rather by degrees than abruptly.

This is a fine large town and I am going to look over the cathedral in a few minutes. When you and Mother come to this continent next time, you will have to come and look over this country for it will be quite worthwhile seeing, but I won't care if I never see it again. Hope you get safely away on the fifth.

With love, Ramsey

For a number of reasons I wanted to remain in London. It was exciting to be at the centre of activities and it would mean a great deal to Ramsey and Basil to have me there when they had leave. But there was another reason, which I did not disclose to anyone. Stuart Thorne, whom I had so greatly admired, had not come for Christmas as I had hoped. I had not even heard from him, for his letter was forwarded to me later when I was at home in Canada.

In order to stay in London I had to have a useful job to help support myself and to contribute to the war effort. For some reason which I never learned, my brothers did not wish me to become a V.A.D., doing voluntary work in the hospitals. With a letter to General Thacker, supplied by

Colonel G.V. White, I applied for a job at Argyle House, Canadian head-quarters in London. At my interview I learned that if I had been able to do shorthand I would have been welcomed with open arms, but not having this skill all they could offer me was a filing clerk's job. A quick decision had to be made, as the last ship to Canada on which women would be allowed to travel, because the North Atlantic was becoming so dangerous, would be leaving in a few days. At this moment a cable arrived from my father, begging me to return home with my mother, as there soon would be important work to be done in Canada. Within a few days I was on the *Scandinavian* with my mother and Mrs Williams sailing from Liverpool for home.

Though the month was January 1917, the sea was quite calm and the voyage was remarkably uneventful until one evening when the stewards began hurrying about fastening heavy blankets over doors and portholes already blacked out. Orders were given that no one was to go on deck. The little ship vibrated as her engines were driven to their greatest capacity.

A pile of crutches at the entrance to the dining salon told the story: the passenger list consisted mostly of permanently injured Canadian soldiers on their way home from the war accompanied by their doctors and nurses. Also aboard was a small group of civilians among whom were a few women, the last to be permitted to cross the ocean until the end of the war. As the rumour spread that an enemy raider, which had been having great success sinking ships in the Atlantic, was in the vicinity, tension grew among the disabled veterans who wanted above everything else to reach home safely.

One of the passengers was the president of the CPR, who, taking charge of the situation, decided that a ship's concert would be the best solution for the increasing alarm. His problem was that the only person capable of leading the singing was secluded in her cabin. With unpleasant memories of the storm in the Irish Sea on my journey to England in November, I had decided that on this voyage I would only leave my cabin to go on deck if the sea was 'as calm as a mill-pond.' To my amazement the door of my cabin opened suddenly and an impressive gentleman appeared, followed by a steward carrying a tray: 'Just take two glasses of this champagne and you will be in splendid shape to play the piano for us.' As he was obviously a person in authority, I felt I had no option but to follow his orders. Putting on my most glamorous gown and taking from my luggage all the hit songs I had gathered up in London, I went to the lounge and took charge of the concert. Many of the soldiers had assembled with their nurses and I sang for them their favourite sentimental songs: 'Keep the Home Fires Burning,' 'Anytime's Kissing Time,' and 'Roses of Picardy.' Then the men themselves took over and, as 'It's a Long, Long Way to Tipperary' drowned out the throbbing of the engines, the audience relaxed and the raider was forgotten.

A few days later the *Scandinavian* was safely in the port of Saint John. All the soldiers who could walk crowded the decks, and as the ship moved closer to the dock there were shouts of delight: they had heard a train's bell and had seen racoon-skin coats – 'Look at the coon coats,' they shouted. They knew now that they were safe at home in Canada.

Soon after arriving home in Pembroke I was again involved in work at the great army camp at Petawawa. There was the usual canteen duty, and when it was learned that I had brought back from London all the popular army songs I was asked to provide a concert. The gunners came to the canteen in hundreds. It was certainly not a plush concert hall but they found it a welcome change from their tents. They sat on long rows of benches facing a roughly constructed stage on which stood an upright piano. This evening, as I stepped onto the stage, I noticed that all the benches were filled.

Taking the precious copy of 'It's a Long, Long Way to Tipperary,' which had been used with such good effect on board the *Scandinavian*, the accompanist went to the piano and played a few bars. As I began to sing, the soldiers began to hum the tune; in a few moments they caught the words and the volume grew. They linked arms across the great hall, swaying in alternate rows, faster and faster, shouting louder and louder, until it seemed to the singer, standing alone on the stage, like a tumultuous, roaring sea. Almost overwhelmed, bracing to withstand a spasm of dizziness, I saw with delight the laughing faces of hundreds of happy boys who had just learned the words to the most famous of all the war songs.

The weeks spent in England had opened our eyes to some of the realities of trench warfare. Adventure and glamour obviously had no part in it. The intelligent young men with whom we had talked over the dinner table in London avoided all reference to the unspeakable horrors and wretched discomforts. These were things they endured. Their only hope and purpose was to survive and bring it all to a successful conclusion.

I found that the letters from France, which had been kept with care, meant even more to me now that I understood better the conditions under which they had been written.

Lieutenant Basil M. Morris

Basil leaving for France –
'all dressed up like a
Christmas tree,' as he said

Bob Murray, Ramsey, and Basil
at Bailleul, 1916, behind the
lines where they met by accident

Grace in London, 1916

Canadian soldiers at the front: a field post office (above); a field kitchen; resting in the trenches

Canadian troops returning home on the *Olympic* after the war

Opposite On the Western Front

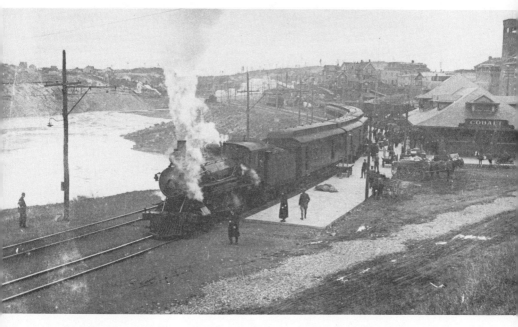

Cobalt, where Stuart managed a mine and Grace holidayed in the summer of 1916

Major Stuart M. Thorne

8 ❈ No more mud ❈ ❈ ❈ ❈ ❈ ❈ ❈

On Christmas Day, 1916, Ramsey and I had dinner with our mother at the Waldorf Hotel in London. At the end of the meal we were joined by several officers from the First Canadian Tunnelling Company, including the new commanding officer, Major C.B. North. My mother was very happy to meet the major, who spoke with enthusiasm of his youngest officer, Basil, and expressed regrets that he was leaving the company. She was not so happy to learn that it was impossible for him to take any steps to prevent his transfer to the Royal Flying Corps.

At this point in the war the enemy had the upper hand in the air, and the British air service was in great need of young officers to train as observers and pilots. A notice had gone out to all officers between the ages of nineteen and twenty-five serving in France to apply for a transfer; the officers commanding their units had been ordered to let them go. If accepted, the new recruit would receive his training in action as an observer over the battle line in France; later he would be sent to England to be trained as a fighter pilot.

Basil was aware that casualties were much greater in the Royal Flying Corps than in the other services, but relief from the mud of the trenches and the wet underground tunnels had become almost an obsession with him. Besides, he longed to serve with men of his own age. His knowledge of machine guns, which he had gained from his six months of training with the 59th Battalion at Barriefield, now stood him in good stead, and he was able to qualify rapidly as an observer.

He had chosen the most glamorous but also the most dangerous branch of the services. The fragile planes were used mostly to fly along the battle-front to observe the enemy installations and direct the fire of the artillery.

The pilot flew the machine while the observer signalled the artillery and also used the machine gun if they were attacked by enemy aircraft; the seats of both airmen were unprotected. The planes were frequently shot down by anti-aircraft guns and the airmen were lost because they had not yet been equipped with parachutes.

Back in the trenches with the Tunnellers for the time being, Basil was anxious to assure his family, especially his father, that he had made the right decision.

9/12/16

Dear Father,

I wrote you a short note from London. My leave is over, worse luck, and I am on my way back to the Company. I haven't mentioned to you before that I intended joining the R.F.C. (Royal Flying Corps) have I? I didn't want to do it until I had decided definitely. The job I have is mighty good, but the other appeals to me too. What do you think of it?

The four of us had a splendid holiday in England and my only regret was that it was not longer and that you were not there as well. I would like awfully to see you again, Father. It does seem so long since I have seen you, doesn't it?

Christmas is nearly here and I wish I were back in Canada for it. We will at least have a regular Christmas dinner as Major North took care of that.

I am sorry I had to cable for more money, but really, being on leave in London twice in a little over a month costs money. You have no conception how fast it goes in England. The tipping is really fierce.

I will let you know soon what I have decided to do with regard to the R.F.C.

Your loving son, Basil

Dec. 9/16

Dear Mother [in England],

I arrived safely but have a long wait here before our train goes up. It is a good job you did not come down with me because we had no wait at the boat at all but got right off the train onto the boat and sailed in less than half an hour.

Probably will have to go up to the trenches tomorrow. Now that I am on my way back I want to get there as these French towns have no charm for me at all. Will write again when I get to camp. Don't worry.

Love, Basil

Dec. 13/16

Dear Father,

I have received all the parcels you have sent up to now and there were some good ones too. The cake was mighty fine, I can tell you and we all enjoyed it very much indeed. We could not keep it until Christmas.

Everything is going fine. I had a fine holiday in England with Mother, Grace and Ramsey. We were up in Scotland for a few days and I really enjoyed it immensely. I have been accepted by the R.F.C. and will likely be called up before long. What do you think of it?

Love, Basil

Dec. 13/16

Dear Mother,

I was down to R.F.C. Genl. Hd. Qts. and have been accepted. I have decided to go there now and really I don't think that I am at all foolish.

The Coy. here pulled off a stunt while I was away which was quite a success. We have been congratulated by the Army for it.

I am going up to the trenches tonight and will be up there for probably a week so don't expect a letter from me for a while.

Lots of love, Basil

19/12/16

Dear Father,

This is really the first chance that I have had to write you a decent letter. I came down from the trenches last night for a few days rest and am glad to be here because it is no fun up in the line these days. The mud is fierce and it is mighty cold and miserable. Not so very long ago we pulled off a good stunt here and certainly pulled it on Fritz besides killing a few of the Huns. It gave us great satisfaction to get him the way we did as it was an uphill fight for us from the start in this section and we are top dog now.

This surely will be the last Christmas that we will be apart like this. I hope so anyway.

I have been accepted into the R.F.C. and likely will have to report any time now. What do you think of it? I cannot see where I am making a mistake although Mother seems to think so.

Over here, everybody is quite cheerful and are a lot more optimistic as to the war finishing soon than they were ever before.

I hope you have a good Christmas.

Your loving son, Basil

19/12/16

Dear Grace,

I got several letters yesterday – one from you, one from Mother and one from Ramsey. I am glad you have located and forwarded my pack although it has not reached me here as yet. However, I hope to see it in the near future.

I have been accepted into the R.F.C. and now am waiting to be called up for it. I should be called up in the course of a few days now.

Love, Basil

Dec. 21/16

Dear Mother,

I am writing this in the mess and hope it gets to you before Christmas. It is an awful day here today, raining and snowing alternately and a heavy wind. I go up to the trenches tonight for a short spell and I expect it will be my last turn up there. I have put the R.F.C. business through and hope you don't mind too much. I am absolutely fed up on the trenches and the mud, and the R.F.C. appeals to me very much. I have not heard a word from Father as to what he thinks about it. My address will be the same until you get further word. I expect any time now to report to the R.F.C.

Don't worry about me.

A Merry Christmas and New Year.

Your loving son, Basil

For Basil, trench warfare had come to an end. At the beginning of January 1917 he was attached to the 6th Squadron, Royal Flying Corps. There would be no more crawling through water in saps and tunnels under no man's land, no more watching for snipers' bullets and carefully judging where the next shell would burst, no more snatching a few hours' sleep in a dugout infested with rats, and, above all, no more mud. He would now take his training as an observer over the line in France. His enthusiasm was rewarded, as the O.C. of his flight gave him every possible opportunity to qualify. In five weeks, instead of the usual two or three months, he had won his observer's wing and would await his turn to be trained in England as a fighter pilot.

France, 8/1/17

My dear Mother,

I am mighty sorry about not sending you my address before. But it was impossible to do so as I am only finally settled today. I have been up several times and surely like this job so far. The squadron that I am in is a very safe squadron and the casualties are not heavy.

My new address is 6th Squadron, R.F.C., B.E.F., France. Honestly, Mother, I am glad I have transferred to this bunch. There are an awful lot of Canadians. I guess pretty nearly half of the officers are Canadians. Honestly, Mother, this is no more dangerous than my last job.

Love, Basil

France, Jan 10/17

Dear Father,

I must say, I am sorry, Father, for not having written to you oftener especially as you must be lonesome with Mother and Grace both away. However, I get pretty lonesome over here too. As you said in a letter to me once, a chap may have friends but there is nothing like his own blood. It does seem funny, Father, but although I scrap with Ramsey and we have tiffs I never feel so close to anyone as to him. I always have the feeling I could trust him absolutely with everything, and he makes a great chum to be with too, even if he is a bit stubborn.

I am now in the R.F.C. alright. You have never told me whether you approved of my changing over or not. Since I have come I really think, Father, that it was a good change. I was awfully fed up on the trenches, the mud and slush and everything.

I have been up several times in the aeroplanes and liked it very much. It is queer but you do not realize the speed you are going at all up in the air unless of course by the wind, but I mean with reference to the ground. It is very interesting picking out points and it is very hard to see a gentle slope.

The machines we have here are big and safe, but not very fast and are used for observation work and bombing, but need to be escorted by a fast machine. I expect I should qualify in about two months' time and then will get back in a month or so to qualify as a pilot.

Being out here as an observer first does a chap a lot of good and besides nearly all the observers here can fly the machines themselves. I am going to get some idea of it too as the machines can be run either from the observer's seat or the pilot's, so that if anything did happen to the pilot I should have a chance. I hope I haven't told you any state secrets.

Mother and Grace should be home by now so give them both my love.

I had a letter from Ramsey today saying he was back in France. I am sorry he is back here and wish he could have stayed in England.

Lots of love, Basil

France, Jan. 10/17

Dear Mother,

I reported to the Squadron here on New Year's Day and have been here learning dope and working fairly hard. I have not done very much actual flying so far but have been learning signalling, machine-gun work and a lot of theoretical work.

I was over to the camp today and saw several of the fellows there but most were up the line. Really, Mother, you have absolutely no idea of the relief to be able to feel that I am not going back up to the trenches again. I simply cannot write it on paper. If you could only feel one part of the dread I was slowly getting of going up to those trenches you would fully appreciate my relief at being away from them. In this job, when you are not flying, you are absolutely safe.

I was awfully sorry I could not write and let you know my address before you sailed. I got your parcel OK and it was very nice. I have had several very interesting letters from Meta Mackenzie [a cousin he met on leave in Scotland] and I like to hear from her.

Love, Basil

Jan. 18/17

Dear Mother,

I am fairly well settled here now and like this job OK. Really, Mother, I am pleased I transferred as this is a jake job and the crowd here are really awfully decent chaps. They all help me which makes it easier as there is a lot of stuff to learn. I have to qualify as an observer first and spend several months out here observing before I can get back to qualify as a pilot.

Jan. 20 – I am sorry, Mother, I did not get this letter finished last night, but I have very little time to write letters. Bob Murray and George Morley have been over this afternoon and I was very glad to see them. They came over about four and stayed to tea. I am very glad indeed that Bob had got the M.C. [Military Cross]. He deserved it. How did you like Major North and Captain Spencer?

I have a fine hut now. There are two of us in it and we have a nice little stove and a couple a good camp beds, and everything fixed up top-hole.

I suppose you are having real winter at home now with a decent amount of snow. I am glad that Grace went home with you as I know she would get quite lonesome if she stayed behind.

Lots of love, Basil

23/1/17

Dear Grace,

We are having a spell of winter weather now and it has been quite cold for about a week and there is a couple of inches of snow. It looks quite like home to see the youngsters sliding on the ponds which are frozen over. I am in my new hut and am with a chap who is very nice. He is a man of over thirty I should say – an awfully decent chap.

I was up on duty this morning and had quite an exciting experience. We had a scrap with a couple of Hun machines and it surely was some scrap. It was great shooting at the blighters and their machine-gun bullets were cracking all around us. I don't think I hit either of them but hope so. It was my first try over the line and so was quite a good initiation. I didn't feel at all nervous up in the air during the scrap but was a bit shaky after we got back. The pilot certainly shot our machine around in all sorts of ways.

Remember me to the girls and my love to Mother and Father.

Lots of love, Basil

Jan. 25/17

Dear Father,

We are surely having some fun here these days. It is regular winter weather, snow and all the ponds frozen over solidly. There is a fair sized pond near our mess, that everyone slides on continually. One of the chaps in one of the other flights has a pair of spring skates which each of us borrowed. They are awfully hard to skate on having curved bottoms, but we had some fun out of it at any rate.

Durkin and myself were out for a ride this afternoon on a couple of horses. It was very nice only the roads were very hard and quite slippery in parts. However, I enjoyed it very much indeed. I was over to my old company for dinner last night and enjoyed it very much. I like going back to see the old crowd once in a while to keep in touch with them. I am mighty glad I am not in the trenches this weather. The poor infantry must be pretty fed up on it.

I had a letter from Ramsey today. He is instructing at the Divisional School for the present which is a fine job. I hope he hangs onto it for a while. He says he will be there until needed for his battalion.

Lots of love, Basil

Feb. 1/17

Dear Mother,

I had my first letter today from you since you left England. It was written on board ship and you seemed to be having a much nicer trip back from what you had coming over.

This new job of mine is OK and I like it. I am nearly qualified now as an observer and so I expect I won't be as long out here as an observer as usual. The weather has been splendid and our flight commander has given a lot of opportunities to me. The work really is very interesting and I like it ever so much better than my other job. Do you know it is two months now since I came back to France.

Your loving son, Basil

4/2/17

Dear Father,

I am quite snug and comfortable sitting here by the fire in my hut. I really neglect you most woefully, but I hope you understand that a letter to any of you at home is meant for you all.

I am practically qualified now with regards to observer's wing and will be completely qualified tomorrow if my luck is good. I have been very lucky indeed in getting my wing so soon but the weather for the past fortnight has been wonderful and I have got my outside work in much quicker than ordinarily is possible. There is a lot of stuff to learn to qualify as an observer, mostly about artillery work, etc. It is really very interesting and I like the work very much indeed. I have no regrets whatever about transferring over here.

We have had real winter here for the past two weeks – steady frost without a break and there is no sign of a thaw.

Must close now, love to all.

Basil

7/2/17

Dear Ramsey,

I got your letter the other day and was very glad to hear from you again. I am practically qualified as an observer now and have managed to do it in pretty good time.

I get so taken up with the work that I never think of the Archie unless of course it comes very close. Those Huns are mighty good shots I assure you and we generally have a couple holes in our machine.

9/2/17

I took my last test this morning and am now a qualified observer. I am afraid though I won't be able to get back to England again to qualify as a pilot for some time as we have to spend considerable time out here first. The work is fine here and I like it very much. It is clean at least and when away from the line we are out of it entirely.

I don't think we have had a dud day for three weeks, and flying every day. It was lucky for me as I got qualified quickly.

There is a very nice restaurant near here that we have dinner at some-times. It is rather a nice place and we were up there the other night. There was a chap there who was on the variety stage. I don't know whether you heard of him, Capper by name. He used to be at the pavil-lion and all the London places.

I hope you hang onto your job as it is a good one. I may get leave again in about a month. Here's hoping.

Love, Basil

9/2/17

Dear Mother,

This won't be a long letter, but just to let you know that I am quite well and in excellent health and spirits. I heard from Father and one from you written on the boat. I am glad to see that you had a better voyage than coming over.

I hear from Ramsey regularly and he has a nice job at the Div'l School. I only hope he can keep it for some time as it is a jake job indeed.

I am qualified now as an observer and am glad to have all my tests off my chest this way.

Do you know that one week from today, I shall have been out in this country for a year. It is a long time in this rotten country, and I am fed up on it, although this flying game is a nice change and I like it very much indeed. I am mighty glad I transferred as I was fed up on the trenches.

I suppose you are getting lots of cold at home now. It has been cold here steadily for over three weeks now, a most remarkable state of affairs. We surely have lots of flying these days.

Love, Basil

20/2/17

Dear Mother,

I am writing this to you before I turn in and so it won't be terribly long because I am rather tired. I have had several nice long letters from you since I joined the squadron and since you have been home. I would tell you all about the squadron and the sort of work we do and so on, but it is against orders to put anything like that in a letter.

Randolph White [from Pembroke] is now a prisoner and slightly wounded. I don't know how it happened or anything, but I guess they were brought down in Hunland.

The last few days have been quite dud and raining so we have had no flying. Now that I have got qualified the more dud weather the better I shall be suited because the summer will be here soon enough and we shall have enough to do then.

I am glad Uncle Osborne [with the Canadian Army Medical Corps] is in England now because I shall be able to see him when I go on leave, which I hope will be before long. However, it may not come for a while yet.

I hear from Ramsey regularly and he seems to be OK. Don't worry about me please as I am OK and will be as lucky as ever I hope.

Lots of love, Basil

23/2/17

Dear Mother,

I am still here and still going strong. We have had a good stretch of dud weather lately and haven't done any work at all. It gets very monotonous indeed this constant inactivity and we are all getting fed up on it. However, when we had that long stretch of fine weather, we were rather tired of it too. What is best is fairly decent weather with a few dud days thrown in to give us a rest now and then.

We have now a number of new observers here and although I only came here about two months or so ago, I am third senior observer in our flight while there are about four or five junior to me. We have a full major here who is an observer and an awfully decent chap. It seems funny having a major just an ordinary flying officer.

I am sorry about Randy White being taken prisoner but I don't think he was very badly wounded. They were brought down and I guess were lucky to come out of it alive.

My hopes get raised one day about leave and dashed to the ground the next. I may go next Sunday or the next Sunday or perhaps not for a month. I don't know until the day before I go. I find it hard to get any money saved now and will have to stop my assigned pay.

I haven't made up my mind yet where I shall go this next leave of mine. I may go to Scotland again but do not know.

I certainly wish you people were to be in England my next leave, but those things only happen once in a while don't they? I surely enjoyed my last leave immensely.

There has been a heavy fog all over for the past few days and it has been very miserable indeed. This sort of weather gives me the creeps and I hate it. We don't have to worry much about mud in this show however.

Lots of love to Father and Grace,

Love, Basil

25/2/17

My dear Grace,

I haven't written to you very much since you got back home but I will try and make up for it in the future and write really often.

I wrote to Uncle Osborne the other day, c/o The Bank of Montreal, but have had no reply from him at all. I would like to hear from him and get his address as I could see him on leave, which I hope may come soon. One never knows when one will get leave here until shortly before one goes. However, there is a rumour that I may go next Sunday. I hope it is true. If it is I shall go with a chap from this flight and likely will spend part of my leave with him at his home in Southampton. That will be a whole lot better than staying in town, won't it? I wish you people were still in England. When I last saw you I had no idea I should have leave so soon again. Do you know it is just about three months since I last saw you. It doesn't seem that long. I have been out in this awful country for over a year now and it doesn't look as if I would get away from it for good sometime yet. Leave is fine and I surely like it, but it is all too short and it is fierce coming back to this god-forsaken country. I certainly felt blue that morning I said goodbye to you and Ramsey at Victoria. We get two weeks leave now in this unit which gives us twelve days in England, and I intend to make the most of my twelve days this time. I wish Ramsey would be there with me. I haven't been on leave yet that I haven't seen Ramsey, so will be rather lost without him.

I am orderly officer today and all the others have gone to a movie show. We had a fire this afternoon in one of the huts, but very little damage was done, but being orderly officer, I had to work at it. It gave a little excitement to things.

I haven't done a tap of work these past two weeks, haven't even been up in an aeroplane for a joyride as the weather has been so bad. Time begins to hang heavy on my hands now and I would like a bit of a change. Probably when the good weather comes though I will get more than enough. I hope it stays dud till I go on leave.

We have been playing a lot of bridge here lately and there are some very good players here, so I am learning a bit more of it.

Bob Murray may go to India with the R.E.'s. They want a number of them and he wants to go. He may change his mind however later, but at present seems quite determined to go. It would be a fine job, and he would see a bit more of the world at the government's expense. I go over to the company quite often as they are fairly close here. We have some fine riding horses in the squadron and I ride over. Roy Spencer wants to be remembered to you and Mother. Don't laugh when I tell you I ride quite a bit, and although by no means an expert rider enjoy it very much and don't get at all stiff. I am learning more all the time too and hope to be a fair rider in the near future. I should like to get a few lessons to break me of any bad habits that I have. How is the shorthand course coming along?

I am awfully sorry about poor Randy White being made a prisoner. It is a lot better than being killed, isn't it? He is only slightly wounded.

We have quite a bunch of officers here now and quite a few new ones and I am by no means junior now. Don't repeat this but so far I hold the record for qualifying in this squadron and none of them qualify nearly so quickly. I did it in five weeks while most of them take two months and usually three. That isn't blowing my own horn but it pleases me muchly. For heavens sake don't repeat it outside of the family, but I just wanted to let you know. I am now a pucker observer and a member of the R.F.C.

I have started to play ground hockey. It really is quite a good game and I like it. It is not hard to pick up at all.

It seems very funny to me now in this company, being no longer looked on as a youngster as I was in the Tunnelling Company. The average age here is about twenty-one. The O.C. of the squadron is only about twenty-five, while our flight commander is not yet twenty-two. They are an awfully decent bunch here and I like them all very much indeed.

Write soon. Lots of love,

Basil

3/3/17

Dear Mother,

I got back to the squadron last night after having been away for a few days. I was attached to a heavy artillery battery for those few days, to get an idea of the running of a battery so that we could keep in closer touch with the artillery. I enjoyed my stay there very much indeed although it was so short, and learned a great deal. It was funny being under shell fire again after having been away from it for so long, and the noise of our own guns firing was something fierce. The battery was very comfortable indeed, and had very nice quarters. They even had a piano in one of the dugouts, which had been looted from somewhere or other. I brought back one of the artillery officers from the battery to see how we do our end of the job, and it is a nice rest for him besides and it will do him good.

I heard from Uncle Osborne this morning and will try and keep in touch with him.

He does not seem to know yet if he will be coming to France or not. If he has any sense he will stay in England, because it is rotten out here in the hospitals even, although out of shell fire.

I am afraid my leave is off once more but it cannot be helped. I am getting a boudoir cap made for Grace which I shall send to her when I go on leave. It is very nice, being made of silk and Flemish lace and I hope she likes it. The lace I may say is washable. You look at that stuff when it comes and see if you can figure out how on earth the women do it. I have often watched girls make lace but I cannot follow it. Confidential: I sent one to Frances [a girl in Pembroke] – don't suppose it was out of the way, was it?

I am rather disappointed today to find out that I am not going on leave with Durkin so I won't get a chance to visit him.

Dinner will be ready in a few minutes so I shall have to close I am afraid, and get washed.

I hope you are having a good time. Lots of love,

Basil

8/3/17

Dear Mother,

You were asking me about the parcels from the church and from Mrs. Dunlop. I acknowledged the church one. I wrote to Miss Beatty, thanking her for it and just got Mrs. Dunlop's parcel yesterday.

We are having a regular March storm here today just like you get at home – lots of wind and snow. The huts we have aren't exactly built for this weather and the snow gets in through the cracks which isn't very pleasant. However it only happens once in a long time and is a mere detail.

Things here have been going along as usual and everything is 'top hole.' I am getting all sorts of English expressions now and will be a bally Englishman before long, I don't think.

The mail has just come in and as usual there is nothing for me. I don't know why it is but I don't get all my mail by any means, I am sure. It is very annoying and I get rather fed up getting a few letters, but I suppose it cannot be very well helped. Bob Murray has decided not to go to India.

I must close,

Love, Basil

9/3/17

Dear Grace,

This won't be a very long letter as I haven't got much news to tell you as everything is going along here as usual.

I was up for a job this morning but it was too misty and we had to come down again. It was quite a nice joyride however, and I enjoyed it. I was to go up again this afternoon but it was still rather dud so I didn't go. I was just as glad as the pilot I was told to go up with isn't greatly to my liking. They are all very good, but of course, we all have our preferences.

It has been snowing steadily all afternoon and is still rather cold, but there should be a change soon. We are all out of coal and our huts are all mighty cold. The only fire we have is here in the mess room so we all hug it pretty closely.

One of our chaps left camp the other day when he was orderly officer without asking permission and as a result got a weeks orderly officer. He is getting mighty sick of it though this is only his third day.

Would you please send me a couple of pounds of Laura Secord chocolates from Toronto every once in a while. They are mighty good.

Love, Basil

10/3/17

My dear Father,

I haven't written to you for some few weeks. You perhaps sometimes think that I don't think of you very much because I don't write often, but I assure you that I do, and it is only because I write to Mother and Grace as often as possible.

We are having a lot of very dud weather lately and consequently have had very little work to do. I don't mind but really this doing nothing gets very boring. I don't like too much flying over the lines but I like a bit of it to keep up my interest.

I haven't been over to see the Tunnellers lately but may ride over tomorrow if it is still dud.

We had a lovely crash on the aerodrome this afternoon but no one was hurt although the machine turned completely over. It was rather funny as both the pilot and observer were hanging upside down in their seats held in by their belts. The fool of a pilot had tried to land downwind, so naturally it happened. He is the only dud pilot that we have in the squadron and will likely have to do more flying alone before he takes up an observer.

I have a gleam of hope about leave now and although it is not definite by any means yet, it is getting closer.

I got an awful scare last night. I was told that I should have to go down south to another squadron to a particularly warm spot, but I am not experienced enough yet and another chap was sent who was longer here. I certainly was glad for two reasons, one that this is a very nice squadron with very decent chaps and another that the place I was going to was rather hot.

I should like very much indeed to tell you all about our work out here as it is very interesting and I am sure it would interest you very much, but I cannot very well. I have written to Stanley Gordon [from Pembroke] to try and have him get leave at the same time as I have it. I haven't seen him for ages now, not since the day we left Pembroke. Do you remember that day? It stands out among my memories. It, and a few others, especially the night I left St. John for England and the morning I went back to France when Grace and Ramsey were down to the station to say goodbye. I also remember very distinctly my first visit to the trenches. That was a funny night and we had to go through water up to our necks in the trenches. Not quite – but nearly! I surely thought I was brave when we walked over the top for a piece, although it was a good eight hundred yards back of the line.

It is very funny here indeed. Everybody is kidding me all the time about my accent, etc. There are two other Canadians here but they both

were Englishmen out in Canada and so aren't pucker Canadians, so I
have to more or less hold the fort alone. They are all an awfully good
bunch though and we have a good time.

Tomorrow is Sunday once more. The weeks certainly pass by here at a
great old rate and one week is past before I scarcely realize that it has
started. The summer and our really hard work will be on before we
know where we are at.

I expect two weeks leave this time, which will surely be rather bon,
won't it? Leave comes around very regularly in this corps, about once in
three months or so. By the time I get my next leave, it will have been
about four months since my last one.

I was not feeling very well for a couple of days last week and stayed in
bed for two days. I think it was a slight touch of influenza which I must
have caught while I was up at the battery. I don't know whether I told
you or not that I was attached to a battery for a few days for instruction.
We do this to keep in closer touch with the artillery. It is a very good
idea and helps both us and the artillery.

The Canadian mail has been very irregular lately and I have had very
few letters from home. Probably some of the Canadian mail boats have
been sunk.

The Canadians in the R.F.C. up till a week or so ago just drew their
former rates of pay, but I understand that we are now to draw regular
R.F.C. pay. I hope so because it will help a lot and will amount to over a
pound a day. It is through now for pilots but I don't know definitely yet
for observers but I should imagine it would be the same.

John Beatty [from Pembroke] tried to get into the R.F.C. but they were
full up at the time that he applied.

I surely am glad that I changed over into this game from tunnelling as
it is much nicer.

Your loving son, Basil

Mar. 15/17

Dear Mother,

We have just had tea and while waiting before getting cleaned up for
dinner I thought I would write a few lines to you to let you know I am
still all OK. I cannot understand what is the matter with the Canadian

mails these days. I haven't had a letter of any sort from Canada now for about two weeks or more. I am not the only one either because all Canadians here are getting no mail from Canada. I am getting very fed up indeed on getting no mail and want a letter in the worst way.

We were all over to one of the divisional concerts last night and it really was a splendid show all through and we enjoyed it very much indeed. They have built a theatre, a large wooden hut holding about four or five hundred men. It was partly a pierrot show but they had also one short skit and one quite long one which was really good and awfully well acted. The principal man is a pucker Canadian in England and surely was good keeping everyone in fits all the time. I am enclosing the programme in this letter as I think it is rather good. After the show we had dinner at quite a fair restaurant. I cannot get to like the French dinners very well though and surely like to get back to England for some decent food.

Canadians attached to the R.F.C. are now getting R.F.C. pay so I am a bloated millionaire now and am drawing six dollars a day all told. It was rather rotten at first though as Canadians were only paid their pay of rank, but this bill was put through in Canada a couple of weeks ago.

I was out for a short ride this afternoon but was not very much in a humour for it and did not go very far. I am going over again to see the chaps in the company as I have not been over there for some time and want to see them again soon. It is nice to keep in touch with them and to see them once in a while.

I don't know whether my leave is off or not now. Leave is closed for a while. I really don't mind a great deal one way or another.

Write often.

Love, Basil

March 15/17

Dear Grace,

I wrote a short letter to Mother this afternoon and am starting this to you now but won't guarantee to finish it today. That is a mere detail however, and you will be lucky if you get it at all. I haven't had any Canadian letters for ages and ages and am getting quite fed up on it. There are no Canadian letters coming into camp at all and it is rotten. I certainly want to hear how the world is going around and if you are still the same as usual. Letters are about our only things to look forward to and I miss them very much indeed. There should be quite a bunch of them waiting somewhere and I will likely get a big bunch at one time when they come through.

I told Mother I was enclosing a programme of a show we were at last night in her letter but forgot to do it so shall slip it in here. The show was really splendid and I enjoyed it immensely, also the dinner afterwards. A change of scenery like that does everybody good and as our flight went en masse it has cheered everyone up.

I am quite pleased today as I have heard that Canadians in the R.F.C. are now getting 6.00 dollars a day which surely is some good news and I can do with it quite easily. I haven't heard from Ramsey for several days now and would like to hear how he is getting along. He may not have had a chance to write but he may get a word through soon.

It really is an awful nuisance trying to write a decent letter when there is no news to put in it like just at present, as we are doing nothing. The weather has been so dud for a long time that we have had very little flying to do.

I hope Mother has not got nervous over me at all, and you might convince her that there is no more need to worry now than when I was in the trenches. Of course I happen to be at war, and these are dangerous but no more now than in the Tunnellers, the only difference being that instead of running the risk of going up, I run the risk of going down. I never realized I could get so calloused about fellows going west as I am and it is the same for everyone.

Vernon Castle has been very badly injured here. He got a direct hit by an anti-aircraft shell, but managed to land somehow which is very extraordinary, but nevertheless is pretty badly smashed up. It isn't a very nice sight seeing a man brought down, but I mustn't mention those things, must I, because they worry you people much more than they do me. We are all fatalists here and don't worry in the least. It is the only way, otherwise life would be miserable.

This letter I am afraid is rather dull and I hope it hasn't bored you to death.

Love, Basil

It was noon on March 17, 1917, that the plane with Basil and his pilot was shot down over Belgium.

These laid the world away; poured out the red
Sweet wine of youth; gave up the years to be
  Of work and joy, and that unhoped serene,
  That men call age: and those who would have been,
Their sons, they gave, their immortality.

Rupert Brooke, *1914 & Other Poems*

The dreaded telegram beginning 'Regret to inform' reached Basil's home on the 19th of March. To my parents and me, it seemed at first unbelievable, but we had to accept the appalling fact that Basil was dead. The tragic news reached Ramsey in the trenches where he was serving with his battalion, the 38th; he wrote to us a few days later from the front.

France, March 27th/17

Dear Father,

I will start this letter now and try and finish it sometime later tomorrow or the next day as I haven't time to write much this time. I have to rejoin the btn. tonight and have for the last few days been to the 6th Squadron R.F.C. and back to find out what I could and let you know re it. It took me two days each way. The O.C. of the 6th Squadron R.F.C. said that they had done some very successful work and he seemed awfully sorry about it. I have been more or less benumbed by the whole thing I believe, Father, which is perhaps better. It is all awfully hard for you but please do what you can for Mother and Grace. It couldn't have been better if death had to come and it perhaps is harder to bear at home than for us who ourselves have to pay the penalty. Please don't worry about me here at all. We are happy here.

I have to get to the btn. by tonight as the permission to go to the 6th Squadron R.F.C. was from the corps and I have to get back as quickly as possible. I was there for several hours and made as careful enquiries as I possibly could. I didn't take their word for everything but went to where the thing happened and asked a few men who saw it about it and have a fairly accurate account of it as far as it is possible to find out. It is as follows: The machine [a BE2D aircraft equipped with Lewis guns] was returning from several hours flying over the lines at noon on the 17th. It must have been struck sometime before starting to come home by a piece of anti-aircraft shell for when, about half a mile from the aerodrome and when starting on the first turn to come down, it crumpled in the air and fell to earth. They couldn't have known about the machine being hit for it was ten miles from the line it happened and it must have happened very suddenly. I also asked re the pilot and he was apparently an old hand at the game and not at all beginning it.

It is much easier for anyone here, Father, as you would understand if you were here, to take what comes to them. You look forward to certain things as inevitable and, if one is severely wounded or anything, it has to come. Having accepted this, life becomes bearable here. Death has no horrors for anyone here, at least for those who have been here a few weeks or more and who have made good here. For this reason I cannot conceive of a worse tragedy, Father, than a wasted life, and one's life here at any rate is not wasted. It is hard enough for one just starting in life as far as that goes, but one who has gone through some months here has had more experiences and has done more than most people can accomplish in a lifetime, and it is a man's work here and not anything else. It is something to have come out here and done what is expected of you, and those who haven't come don't come into the matter at all. This is a matter purely among men and the men are here. It's the state of the world just now and this upheaval of everything in life and of anything that counts in life, that makes it necessary. It is an extraordinary state of things and we have to do what we can, if it's the hardest thing to do in the world that we will ever have to do. Let us hope that the world after will be better for it.

Please give my love and sympathy to Mother. Do what you can for her. Also give my love and sympathy to Grace. It is harder for them perhaps than it is for me as I am still here and have the chance to do what I can. If you can send Mother some place for a change mightn't it be better? I have avoided being by myself after the first day or two as much as possible as I couldn't stand it. It is all right now though as I know what I have to do. I wrote to you a few days ago and hope you received it all right as I wrote in such a hurry and all that. I don't remember much about it just now, but I believe I wrote it just the day or so before I went to Belgium. I will write the rest of this some other time but I must get on to the company now.

I have written the last part of this at the horse lines. The company are not in the trenches just now for a few days. I will write and enclose a few things when I get a chance, any more information I can think of and anything else.

With deepest sympathy and love for all of you.

I am, your loving son – Ramsey.

Finally spring came to Flanders. Flowers began to bloom again in the desecrated fields, and birds sang in the bright sky above.

9 ❈ The last battle ❈ ❈ ❈ ❈ ❈ ❈ ❈ ❈

It was not easy to recover from the shock of Basil's death. At the battle-front the soldiers accepted death as a fact of war, as 'part of the game.' As Ramsey put it in his letter to our father, certain things were 'inevitable' and had to be accepted: it was better to do a man's job and 'pay the penalty' than to lead 'a wasted life.'

But at home we closed our minds to such a possibility. In spite of the long casualty lists that appeared day after day, we believed our loved ones led charmed lives. It seemed to be the only way we could do what was required to help bring the struggle to an end.

Ramsey's explanation of the soldiers' point of view helped us to accept the blow and to realize that there was still much to be done to make sure that the precious lives had not been wasted. If it was 'a war to end wars,' as the soldiers believed, then this was not a time to sit and mourn.

Within a few weeks another dark cloud of anxiety lay over the family as the 38th Battalion took part in the great assault on Vimy Ridge. In the early hours of April 9, Easter Monday, backed by sleet and snow and a driving wind, fifteen thousand Canadians advanced in the first wave behind a steady artillery barrage towards the German positions on the ridge; a second and a third wave of infantry followed. In this battle the Canadian Corps wrested from the enemy one of the most formidable defensive positions on the Western Front. It was a great victory, but the casualties were severe. It seemed too much to endure until we learned that Ramsey had survived.

It was then that our cousin, General Alex McDougall, asked for Ramsey's transfer to his unit, the Canadian Forestry Corps, and sent him to a camp in the north of Scotland; the loss of one son, and Ramsey's

ordeal at Vimy Ridge, seemed to him enough for one family to suffer for
the time being. We were greatly relieved, because it meant that Ramsey
was effectively out of action. Although he was doing essential war work in
the north, he wanted to get back to the front; but he was still serving with
the Foresters when the war ended. Before returning to Canada he
attended lectures at Oxford University to prepare him for taking up his
studies once again.

By the end of 1917 the opportunity came for us to play our part on the
home front. Great losses had been suffered by the Canadian expeditionary force at Vimy Ridge and other battles, and the casualties had to be
replaced. One important province, Quebec, was not contributing its share
and so conscription seemed inevitable. In the riding of North Renfrew my
father had been chairman of the Conservative Association for a number
of years; like most Canadians he realized that a coalition government
would be necessary to bring in such a controversial measure. When the
Union government was finally formed in October under Sir Robert
Borden, a general election automatically followed; in North Renfrew a
Liberal, Mr Herbert Mackie, agreed to run for the new government.

For the first time women would be allowed to vote, but they would be a
very select group – the mothers, wives, and sisters of the men in the overseas forces. The job my father had chosen for me, which he had had in
mind many months before when he begged me to return from England,
was to organize the women voters of the riding. Upon my return I had
taken a course in Isaac Pitman shorthand from a nun at the convent, and I
asked several of my friends who had been in the business class there to
help me form a committee. We were provided with a well-equipped office
on Main Street in Pembroke. Through the nominal rolls of the overseas
units we learned who the voters would be and we got in touch by mail
with every one of them throughout the large riding. There were no
women's meetings called, but it was explained to all of them by letter that
the only way they could hope to see their men again was to vote for the
Union government and conscription.

On the night of the election, December 17, 1917, people crowded the
armouries to hear the results, which came first by telephone in the riding
and then by wire from the rest of Canada. The tension was great and angry
looks were exchanged; but we had the great satisfaction of having helped
to elect a coalition government that would bring in conscription, which we

felt was our way of helping to win the war. We expressed our delight in loud cheering and scornful looks for the group of young men who did not like the results.

Although Basil was dead and Ramsey was safely in Scotland, the war continued to affect all our lives. We knew plenty of young men still fighting in the trenches, and letters and parcels continued to cross the Atlantic.

Throughout the war, the letters of one soldier in particular had intrigued me. It was always an exciting day when the box at the post office contained letters from the battlefront. But for me, on occasion, there would be a letter in what I considered to be an attractive hand, always without the formality of 'Miss' on the envelope. Why did he do this? If nothing more, his informal style increased my interest in his personality.

The writer was Stuart Thorne, whom I had first met in the fall of 1915 when he came to Pembroke with the First Canadian Tunnelling Company. His letters were infrequent, usually short, but I always treasured them.

France, March 18/16

Dear Grace,

Thank you very much for the sweater. It was very good of you to go to so much trouble. We have been having miserable weather since we got to France, so that it will be very useful.

I don't care much for the war from a closer view. It is quite a dangerous affair and I don't see how we are going to keep our nominal roll and various papers right with all these shells and other projectiles flying around.

Stuart

July 13/16

Dear Grace,

I have been more or less sick for the past month and am only now feeling right again – got a bad dose of trench fever and couldn't get over it without complications. I got my leave and went to London; spent part of it in hospital and the rest of the time had rheumatism so badly that I could hardly walk.

I hear the Foresters' Btn. has arrived in England and are proceeding to the front (of Scotland). I wish I was a lumberman instead of a miner.

Thanks for your good wishes on my promotion to a captain which rank I am afraid is my limit for this war.

Sincerely, S.T.

Sept. 26/16

Dear Grace,

We are still stuck in the same place, but all the Canadians have left this vicinity and have gone south to the Somme. We hear that they have done exceedingly well there but have suffered heavy casualties, which I suppose is to be expected in the sort of fighting they are doing.

We have only about 20% of our original company left now. Our casualties from the enemy's fire, etc. have been light but sickness is the trouble.

Simpson was killed about a month ago.

S.T.

Jan. 2/17

Dear Grace,

Thank you for your letter from London. I hardly think I will be in England before the end of February but hope you will still be there, in which case you will probably have more than a glimpse of me.

Basil left us last week for the flying corps and I am sure he will like it and do well with them as he is just the right age and weight.

On New Year's Day, Jeff and I were looking back a year and remembering our famous trip from Pembroke to the sea.

Let me know if you are staying in London.

S.T.

May 24/17

Dear Grace,

Have just got back from two months' leave in England which I spent with my sister who is still in London.

Went to Crowboro for two days. It is the Canadian Engineering Camp, filled with officers all of whom are fed up with life and want to get over to France.

I can remember when we left for England in January, 1916, the great expectations we all had of the training we would get in England. We had a great awakening on our arrival and found that nobody knew or cared about us. It is still much the same and unless a man can make a job for himself he has nothing to do.

Jeffery, Murray, Morley, Maxwell, Spencer and myself are all of the officers who came over still with the company. Rogers is in Canadian Corps working on light rys. and is said to have done 1st class work. He refuses to take leave on the theory that if nobody took leave the war would be over so much sooner. Most of us work on the theory that the more leave you get the less chance there is of being hurt.

My sister is still in London and is now working at St. Dunstans (the blind man's home). She likes the work immensely and I am glad to have her there. I wish you had been able to stay in London last winter. I was out of luck not having my leave when you were there.

We are having very fine weather and the traffic on the roads is tremendous. I have never seen anything like it and can't help but feel how tame and uninteresting things will be after the war for the men who have been up in the fronts of the armies. The trees are all out and this gives one a sense of security which one doesn't have in the winter with the enemy looking down on us from the high ground. There are hundreds of airplanes up every day. Yesterday I saw two of them fall. There is surely more individual bravery in the air than in any other branch of the army and you must be proud that Basil played his part in such a glorious service.

Sincerely, S.T.

Stuart, too, was to play his part. For many months the Germans had occupied the high ground in the southern part of the Ypres salient. The battle to dislodge them began in April when the Canadians took Vimy Ridge. This was followed two months later, on June 7, 1917, by the attack on Messines Ridge. Before the battle took place, great mines had been driven into the long, low hill and filled with six hundred tons of high explosives; the First Canadian Tunnelling Company alone laid a single charge of forty-eight tons of explosives 125 feet down at St Eloi. All nineteen mines under the ridge were fired at one time: the ground shook with the violence of the blast, and great sheets of flame rose high in the air. In one day, on a front of ten miles, a ridge long considered impregnable had been demolished. For nearly two years a battle had been going on underground, a battle of miners. In this last, supreme effort, Major Stuart M. Thorne had greatly distinguished himself by preparing the largest of the mines: he was awarded the Military Cross and the Croix de Guerre.

Sept. 18/17

Dear Grace,

We are still very much in the war and notwithstanding the successes of this spring and summer the end doesn't seem to be much closer.

You ask for what great deed I got the Croix de Guerre and I propose to let you into the secret. The French government says to the English army, 'Here are a few decorations for you.' Headquarters of the English army distribute these amongst several armies; then these army authorities distribute them to different branches, and the end of the matter is that somebody must be selected to put the thing on and in this case the Controller of Mines, 2nd army, probably said to himself, 'I had better give this to 1st Tunnelling Co. Who in that company hasn't got much to show? Oh, give it to Thorne and let it go at that.'

We started another attack this morning. A string of wounded Austrians and Germans have been passing down all day. The Germans are mostly young boys. The war now is nothing but artillery. Everything else is secondary. It would probably surprise you to see the German prisoners coming down after being captured. Most of them (if not wounded) are used in carrying down stretchers with our wounded. Others wander down by themselves with nobody paying any attention to them, asking their way and being directed. The most interesting part of an attack is the work of the airmen. They fly forward over the infantry and keep in contact, as they call it, with the enemy, signal by wireless to the guns, also by light signals and machine-gun reports. This morning was a very bad day for them, very cloudy and foggy, but it has cleared up to some extent this afternoon.

Yours, S.T.

Dec. 2/17

Dear Grace,

Your letter reached me a few days ago, and I was glad to hear all the Pembroke news and wish I could be back for a few days to enjoy the fox-hunting without the fox. You are indeed getting very strenuous when you ride thirty miles for the sport of it – living as we do here would be a pleasant rest for you.

Well, I didn't need to go into such details of the winning of the Croix de Guerre, did I? Of course if you want to believe 'The Montreal Star' well and good – that is the great thing about these honors, nobody will believe you when you tell them how you get them and you always get the benefit of any doubt in your favor. Your friends read great accounts in the newspapers and you don't dare to say anything yourself for fear of spoiling your reputation. After a while however you learn that it is quite safe to tell the truth about it, as nobody will believe you anyway.

We haven't been having many dances lately, but had a masquerade dance at one of the Canadian hospitals on Hallow eve, which was quite a success. Some of the costumes were remarkably good. The day before yesterday I rode a motorcycle to St. Omar – about twenty-five miles – got some — there and had a dance that night at one of the hospitals. We left at 11 p.m. to ride back by moonlight over very bad roads and had nothing but bad luck all the way home. One of the men got a puncture about half way home and he and I spent all night in trying to repair and change tires – every one we put on refused to hold up until finally my patience was completely exhausted and I left him to sleep in an ambulance while I went home which I reached at 6 a.m. after sliding all over the road. Riding a motorcycle on muddy pavé roads is about as bad and nerve exhausting a thing to do as I know. However as a result of this effort I got some lace and am sending you a collar which I hope you will like. I haven't any idea whatever if you wear such things in Canada but hope for the best.

Geo. Morley was quite badly wounded about a week ago – a piece of shell tore the muscles and broke the bone of his right arm just below the shoulder. I was with him at the time and had quite a job getting him out to the dressing station but managed to do so without further trouble. The stretcher-bearers, as a result of a close shell dropped the stretcher and George to the ground. It must have hurt him like the devil but he never whimpered over it. He went to England yesterday and will go back to Canada when he is able.

You will have heard that Murray is on his way back. At present Maxwell, Jeffery and myself are all the originals left.

We are all much interested in the Canadian elections. I don't think there is much doubt of the men at the front being in favour of the Union government. It is the only thing to do and we should have had conscription at the start. The party system of government is a failure in a great national crisis. The politicians in general are too narrow minded to see anything beyond the interests of their party and the few good men have their hands so full with the rest without being able to lead the country. We get there in the end but there is a lot of lost motion in the process.

I hope you had a good trip to Toronto. A change of scene is very necessary once in a while and I would be glad to change mine anytime the army sees fit. Things are gradually getting quieter on our front and we may have a peaceful winter.

Give my love to your mother and wish her a Merry Christmas and a happier New Year than the one we are finishing.

Yours very sincerely,
Stuart M. Thorne

Jan. 8/18

Dear Grace,

We have had a move since I last wrote you and have moved down with our own people about 40 miles south. The change is all for the good in every way. The work is in chalk instead of clay and no water to contend with. There are many old mine workings and villages all badly knocked to pieces. Another advantage of the country is that, compared to where we left, there is no shelling and what little there is is all small stuff which, after the 8 and 10 inch shells we have become used to, seem about like Xmas crackers compared to giant firecrackers.

We are all glad over the election results. Almost 90% of the men over here voted for the government, which speaks well for the morale of the Canadian forces.

Sincerely, S.T.

In the spring of 1918 all hopes were pinned on the arrival in Europe of the American army. The United States had finally declared war on Germany in April 1917 and was now at last prepared to enter the conflict on a grand scale. For the enemy it was a most critical period, their last chance to win victory before the Americans arrived in force to tip the balance. Chilling news reached Canada that a great 'push' had started and that the Germans had broken through the line on the British front.

As Stuart observed in his letters, a change in style of fighting was taking place on the Western Front. The emphasis was shifting from infantry to artillery. Since an ever-increasing supply of shells for the Allied guns was essential, light railway engineering battalions were formed to build railway tracks to ensure that ammunition was delivered as quickly as possible to the front lines. It was a type of work at which Canadians excelled. The role of mining, too, was changing, and Stuart sometimes found himself with too much time on his hands.

April 3/18

Dear Grace,

As you will know before this reaches you, the great battle of the war has started and by the time this reaches you a decision will probably have been obtained by one side or the other.

We are on the extreme north flank of battle so far and have not been in action as yet. A week ago when the Germans attacked Arras, we were all ready to take up our positions but were not called on as the enemy attack failed and was beaten back. It seems strange to be on the edge of a huge battle and have nothing to do, but that is almost our position. Our mining work is stopped and we are digging trenches against a possible if not probable attack. We get little news except from the daily papers. In fact probably you get news faster and more accurately than we do, even though we are almost in the battle.

Our work has changed. Mining in an offensive and defensive way is a thing of the past due to both sides changing the way of manning the trenches. Now the front line trench is regarded as an outpost, and in walking along it you only find a sentry perhaps every 100 yards or so. The battle positions are too far back to reach by mining in a reasonable time and the results are not worth the time, labour and material. This is quite a long lecture, isn't it? I had better not exhaust your interest all at once.

I had quite a good trip to Nice in January. The weather here was miserable so that just to be in the warm sun for 10 days leave was enough. Quite a few Canadian officers were at Nice at the time and there was lots of food and plenty to drink – but no music. There is practically no music anywhere in France, in contrast to London, as you know; a mistake, I think, as there is nothing like music to buck up your feelings when you need it, as anyone who has marched with a band knows.

I wish I could get back to Canada. Perhaps before the end of the year we may all be back. In the meantime, it is something to look forward to.

With love, Stuart

May 20/18

Dear Grace,

I have been wandering about what is called the forward area all morning, watching enemy shells explode in the distance. You can imagine how tired of the whole business one gets at times and what a great longing one has for an end to the whole miserable business.

While we were actually mining against the Germans in front of the trench lines there was always an element of excitement to keep up the interest. You had an objective to get to, to keep him from getting under your trenches, and the uncertainty of the whole operation held one's interest. The Germans have made no very serious attacks for a month but are expected to put on another in the next few days.

S.T.

Aug. 10/18

Dear Grace,

Received your letter a few days ago but have been so busy moving around for the past months that I have hardly had time to do anything but eat, sleep and move. The Tunnelling Company has been disbanded and I am now in the 5th Battalion Canadian Engineers, 2nd Division. We have been in the advance east of Amiens which you will have heard about and I am writing this in a broken-down village which the Huns left in a hurry yesterday. The last week on the whole has been the most interesting time I have had since coming to France. Being up with the front of a big attack and going forward behind it is quite a new experience. We are moving ahead from day to day, sleeping in the field or anywhere and strange to say, everybody seems in better spirits. So long as things go ahead and we are going into ground that has been taken from the enemy everything is fine.

S.T.

Aug. 24/18

Dear Grace,

It is a peaceful summer day here with no sign of war. For a few nights the bombing from aeroplanes was very bad so each man immediately he settles down for the night digs out a little hole for himself and sleeps in it.

The French are wonderful and seem to accomplish results with so little effort as compared to our own people. Somehow our attacks seem most ponderous affairs.

S.T.

Armistice was declared on November 11, 1918. On the battlefields of Europe the guns at last ceased firing, and in the amazing silence of the trenches the soldiers waited. The fighting had gone on for so long – month after month, year after year – that at first we could not believe that men were no longer being killed. The relief was almost overwhelming.

Early that morning in Pembroke, a cold, bleak morning with a little snow sifting down, a whistle blew. It was a train whistle at the CPR station. It blew loud and long and people stirred in their sleep. Loud whistles at the two lumber mills on the waterfront joined in, and then the brazen clang of the firebell on top of the town hall. Everybody was now awake. As the bells of all the churches and the sirens at the factories were added to the din, lights appeared everywhere and people poured into the streets. We rushed about visiting friends, laughing and embracing one another, attending spontaneous breakfast parties. By midday a parade had been assembled with every available vehicle, the ancient red and brass fire engine buried under masses of small boys. The riders from Mr Williams' stable, myself among them, rode in an endless procession up and down Main Street. The partying and parading ended only when evening came and fatigue took over.

Although the war ended in 1918, it was the following year before the Canadian forces began returning home. Some of the troops were with the army of occupation in Germany; others were held in England because of a shortage of transportation, resulting in some riots in the army camps amongst men impatient to get home now that their job was done. Stuart put in some time at an infantry school near Boulogne, and then rejoined his battalion in Germany.

Nov. 18/18

Dear Grace,

We have been moving ahead rather quickly and somehow it seems very difficult under the conditions to get settled and composed, so that of late I haven't managed any letters at all. A week ago, I left the battalion and came to 1st Army Infantry School which is just outside Boulogne on the coast. You say 'What does he want to go to an infantry school for now that the war is over?' I had a chance to take the course and as I was feeling tired out, generally worn out and useless, I thought the regular life at a school would do me good and so far I am enjoying the life and feeling better in every way. Every sort of sport is available. I am confining my attention to golf, tennis and bridge so far but am almost enthusiastic enough to play football.

The military end is pretty stiff. In the Tunnelling Company we worked for two years with practically no drill whatever so that getting into an infantry course with a lot of infantry officers naturally one feels that he may do something desperate. I wish I had been able to take this course two years ago. Expect to finish here in about four weeks and will then probably have to find the battalion somewhere in Germany. It is certainly some job to find your division and battalion – nobody knows where they are. You move around in a sort of vague way, asking R.T.O. (Railway Traffic Officers) who never know very much and don't take time to inform you of what they do know.

I hope to get back to Canada by spring. The Canadian Corps seem enthusiastic over the idea of being in the army of occupation, or rather the people at the head of it are, but I don't think the men will care about it for long. It is going to take some time to get the army absorbed into ordinary life again and things normal.

I am wondering what I will do when this army life is over. Somehow I don't feel like going back to Cobalt. What I should do as a mining engineer is to get a connection in England and a job then in S. America, Russia or some other place, but I don't feel like living in a strange country anymore, and think I will go back to Canada just as soon as I can. If the engineers are kept in France to repair the damage done by the Germans in the last two months, I expect to be here for the rest of my life. I am hoping to see you before next summer at latest.

S.T.

Jan. 6/19

Dear Grace,

I returned to the battalion about Christmas and found them, after a trip of five days, at this place, which is on the west side of the Rhine and about twenty miles from Cologne. The army of occupation is almost as unexciting an occupation as you can possibly imagine, and everybody is well fed up with it and anxious to start on the move back.

We don't know yet whether we will be going back to England or whether we will get a boat direct from France. I think we should be back in Canada sometime in April if all goes well.

It is just three years since we left. What a lot has happened in those three years. Looking back, I remember how I enjoyed the month we spent in Pembroke, the best month in the whole three years. I have only three men of the lot who were in Pembroke left with me now.

Stuart

Yvoie, Belgium
April 3/19

Dear Grace,

We are expecting now to leave here for England on April 9th by way of Le Havre, and should get away from England in about a month or early June. Don't waste time worshipping heroes. There are too many and usually they don't turn out to be heroes after all.

Stuart

One day, to my surprise and delight, I received a letter from Toronto.

May 21/19

Dear Grace,

I arrived back in Canada safely last Sunday and am already beginning to feel as if I had never left it. Seeing all my old friends again seems just like being transported to a new world as indeed it is.

We left France on April 14th, stayed at Witley Camp in Surrey till May 10th when we sailed for Canada on the Olympic being the first troops of the 2nd division to get away. The boat was very crowded, 6,500 troops on board, but quite comfortable after the first two days. Landed in Halifax last Friday. We got a fine send-off from Southampton and a great reception in Halifax so everybody was happy.

I hope to see you all before long.

Stuart

When a letter arrived a short time later, asking if he might come to spend a weekend at my home in Pembroke, I felt sure that this would be a visit of sympathy because Basil had been his brother officer. However, I put on my most becoming dress and prettiest hat to meet him at the station. At the end of a few happy and exciting days he proposed marriage. We planned to be married as soon as he was discharged from the army and had found a place again in his profession of mining engineering.

Before undertaking a strenuous job, a doctor in Toronto suggested he should enter hospital for an examination to locate the source of a continual feeling of fatigue. Nothing definite was found, but it was recommended that he take a holiday in Florida with his uncle Mr A.E. Osler. When he returned to Toronto in the spring of 1920 he accepted the position of mine manager for a new mine being opened up by the Trethewey company in Gowganda in northern Ontario. I was not at all deterred when he told me he could offer only complete isolation, and for entertainment a canoe on a nearby lake. It seemed to me a most wonderful adventure.

The rough, strenuous life took its toll after a few months and he began to doubt whether he was strong enough to carry it through. At his request I went to Cobalt and spent a few days as a guest of Mary Rogers, while he came down from Gowganda to discuss the situation with me. We walked over the rocky hills and one evening, in bright moonlight, we found ourselves on a foot-bridge close to what had once been Cobalt Lake but was now filled by 'tailings' of the Nipissing Mine. Almost a moonscape, it gleamed like quicksilver, and reminded Stuart of an incident that had happened to him during the war. His unit had been 'dug-in' in a cemetery in France when suddenly the enemy subjected them to an intense artillery bombardment, showering them with skulls and bones and splinters of ancient coffins. It had been horrible – the living and the dead all mixed up – and it remained in his mind as his most gruesome experience of the war. He felt that perhaps he should not have told me about it, but to share the memory with me was a relief.

When I realized the pressure under which he had been living, I offered to marry him the next day in Cobalt and go into the mine with him at once. As the log cabin being built for us was not ready, he could not accept my offer, but he asked me to travel with him as far as Earlton where he would take a car for thirty miles over rough roads into the mine-site. I went with him to Earlton, and with anxiety said goodbye to him on the railway platform; then I returned to Cobalt on a 'down' train an hour later.

Preparations for my arrival were going forward, the cabin nearing completion, when disaster struck in the form of a great forest fire. For days Stuart and his men fought to save the mine workings, but finally he was overcome with exhaustion and had to be taken south to a hospital. There it was found that he had a mysterious and unusual illness which the doctors were unable to diagnose, but they assured him that with rest he would recover. They advised him to give up his mining career and find less strenuous work.

After returning to Pembroke I received this letter, on August 8, 1920.

36 Summerhill Gardens
Toronto, Ontario

Grace dear,

I wish I was back with you this morning instead of here in Toronto – last week all seems like a bad dream with bright intervals when I was with you. The trip to Gowganda and the return I don't ever want to think about if I can help it, only your part of the trip to Earlton and the bright picture of what might have been had I been able to take you in with me and stay in there. That was not to be.

Your trip to Cobalt has been a tragedy, dear, except that you understand things so much better than you would have had you never come up. Your love means everything to me.

Yesterday, I saw my cousin Dr. Gwyn and will probably take his advice and go to the hospital to give him a chance to keep me under observation, and do what he tells me for at least a month, and then if I could only carry out the plan we thought of and go to Pembroke to work with your father for perhaps six months, everything would turn out as we hoped, dear.

Whatever may happen I have had a few hours in heaven with you and I will always be able to look back to them as my share of happiness.

Write me, Grace, and tell me all about what is happening.

God bless you, sweetheart,
Stuart

Stuart did come to spend several months at my home in Pembroke. A symptom of his illness was a persistent cough, which my mother diagnosed as bronchitis and treated as she had always done with her children; she made sure also that he had nourishing food and plenty of rest. The result of her nursing was a great improvement in his general health, and in the spring he accepted a job with Ontario Hydro. He found and rented a pretty little house with a garden at Niagara-on-the-Lake.

Our future now looked bright and we planned our wedding for the month of June. The day approached and only the last-minute details remained to be completed: final fittings for the wedding dress, invitations to be mailed to close friends. Arrangements for our wedding trip to Quebec City were to be made by the groom on a weekend in Toronto; beautiful roses sent to the bride expressed the joyousness of the approaching day.

It was while attending church with his aunt during his weekend in Toronto that Stuart collapsed. A heart specialist was called and at last the source of his fatigue was diagnosed. Stuart was dying of endocarditis, an infection in the lining of the heart, resulting from his attack of trench fever at the front in the late spring of 1916; the doctor said: 'He has been killed in action just as if a German bullet had pierced his heart.' Because penicillin had not yet been discovered there was no possible cure.

Is all this a dream? A glimmering through the dream of things that were? Or is it the shadow of a dream? The room is filling, mostly with young people. It is heavy with the perfume of masses of flowers. The clergyman, handsome in his white surplice, stands close to the young officer, who appears to be asleep. His eyes are closed. On his khaki tunic gleams a row of bright ribbons. Voices are hushed, the service begins. The words are beautiful, but they are not the words I expected to hear at my wedding. Everything is confusing. It must be the shadow of a dream. Now it is finished. They go away.

Alone I wander to the edge of the country, into a quiet valley where a stream flows gently. I sit near the water and listen to its murmuring. Is it deep enough?

The hours slip by. I am alone still, but the anguish is subsiding. The evening sunlight pours through the golden leaves of the delicate birches; I feel overwhelmed by its beauty. In this tragic world there must be a purpose. Perhaps for me it is that I must live to see that the names of the men who gave their lives for this beautiful country should not be forgotten.

Epilogue

When the war was over, and so many of the people closest to her were gone, Grace Morris had a sense of not belonging in a world that had changed too much. With her father's encouragement she decided to pursue the career in architecture she had sought before the war. Through the head of the School of Architecture at the University of Toronto, a friend of her father's, she was introduced to the Toronto firm of Craig and Madill as an apprentice architect, helping to design houses. At the time she was the only female architectural draughtsman in Toronto, the first woman to work in architecture in the city. Her success brought her membership in the Heliconian Club, in which she has had a deep interest now for over fifty years.

On December 29, 1923, Grace Morris married James H. Craig, one of the partners in Craig and Madill. In time, she left the business to raise their three children, James, Mary, and Sheila.

Jim Craig was a soldier. In the Great War he had been a young officer in command of 'C' Company of the 5th Canadian Light Railway Battalion. The 'Railroad Brigade' built narrow-gauge railways to take ammunition and supplies to the front lines; on return trips wounded soldiers were gathered at collecting stations and brought down to field ambulances. Twenty-five years later, at the age of forty-nine, Major Craig went to war again, to fight a war in Europe that he and his wife considered to be a continuation of the first one. After a year and a half of service in Canada, he was asked to go to England in 1942 to help set up the Canadian Armoured Corps Reinforcement Unit. During her husband's absence for almost three years, in the midst of caring for three teenagers, Grace Craig was at last able to develop her talents as an artist, painting pictures of outstanding quality. Despite Jim's apparent good health, the war work was too strenuous for him at his age; he developed angina, which eventually led to his death.

Canadians do not think of themselves as a military people. Yet all the men in Grace Craig's life have been soldiers. What they were fighting for is perhaps best expressed in the scroll sent to the Morris family when their youngest son Basil was killed over Belgium in the spring of 1917:

'He whom this scroll commemorates was numbered among those who, at the call of King and Country, left all that was dear to them, endured hardness, faced danger, and finally passed out of the sight of men by the path of duty and self-sacrifice, giving up their own lives that others might live in freedom.

'Let those who come after see to it that his name be not forgotten.'